GALAPAGOS

GALAPAGOS

TEXT BY
BARBARA RADCLIFFE ROGERS

PHOTOGRAPHY BY
STAN OSOLINSKI / MARVIN L. DEMBINSKY
PHOTOGRAPHY ASSOCIATES

ADDITIONAL PHOTOGRAPHY BY
JULIETTE ROGERS

MALLARD
PRESS

An imprint of BDD Promotional Book Company, Inc.
666 Fifth Avenue
New York, New York 10103

A FRIEDMAN GROUP BOOK
Published by MALLARD PRESS
An imprint of BDD Promotional Book Company, Inc.
666 Fifth Avenue
New York, New York 10103

Mallard Press and its accompanying design and logo are trademarks
of BDD Promotional Book Company, Inc.

ISBN 0-792-45192-9

GALAPAGOS
was prepared and produced by
Michael Friedman Publishing Group, Inc.
15 West 26th Street
New York, New York 10010

Editor: Sharyn Rosart
Art Director: Robert W. Kosturko
Designer: Lynne Yeamans
Photography Editor: Christopher Bain
Production Manager: Karen L. Greenberg

Photographs © Stan Osolinski/Marvin L. Dembinsky Photography Associates

Typeset by: Mar+x Myles Graphics, Inc.
Color separation by Universal Colour Scanning, Ltd.
Printed and bound in Hong Kong by Leefung Asco Printers Ltd.

DEDICATION

To the people of Ecuador, past, present, and future, in appreciation for their farsighted and unselfish efforts to protect and preserve these islands and their wildlife so that the whole world may continue to study and delight in their riches.

A · WORD · OF · THANKS

Any book on Ecuador is sure to be written with the help of many people, for nowhere are people friendlier or more helpful and hospitable than they are in this beautiful and richly diverse land. It is impossible to name all those who made travel and research easier and more enjoyable, but a few people took extra time and trouble to explain, to interpret, and to help. To them I extend a wholehearted thank you.

To Alejandro Ponce Noboa, president of Galatours in Guayaquil, for his continued hospitality both in Guayaquil and on board the M/V *Bucanero*. Without his help, this book would have been impossible.

To Doris Welch of Galapagos Center in Coral Gables, who provided the most complete information on current studies of the Galapagos from her extensive library and who made all our travel arrangements, and to Marcelo Roman of Ecuatoriana Airlines.

To Captain Juan Angel Cevallos and the staff of the M/V *Bucanero*, especially to First Officer Rolando Garcia Pazmino and Second Officer Nelson Crespo, our appreciation for their patient answers to our endless questions about the sea and the islands.

To Luis Die, the *Bucanero*'s naturalist-guide, who pointed out and explained the details of the islands' wildlife.

To our traveling companions, especially Jean Welch for her unfailing good humor and good company and Maria Gross, of the International Oceanographic Foundation in Miami, for her knowledge of the sea and its bird life, and for sharing it so generously.

And to Julie Rogers, photographer and travel companion extraordinaire, for her tireless work and her sense of humor, both of which made our adventures together in the Galapagos more enjoyable and rewarding.

My appreciation also to Willie Hofmann of the Keene (NH) Public Library for his bloodhound instincts in tracking down and obtaining out-of-print books and references, to Rebecca Trujillo of Galapagos Center for help with translations, and to Lura Rogers for typing a good part of the manuscript.

DEDICATORIA

A la gente del Ecuador; pasado, presente, y futuro. Con apreciación infinita por su gran visión y disinteresado esfuerzo por proteger y preservar estas islas y mantener su riqueza natural para que el mundo entero pueda continuar estudiando y deleitándose con este; "Patrimonio de la Humanidad".

UNAS · PALABRAS · DE AGRADECIMIENTO

Seria virtualmente imposible haber completado un libro sobre el Ecuador sin haber contado con la valiosa ayuda de un sinnúmero de personas que nos brindaron su ayuda incondicional dentro de un marco de cálida hospitalidad, tan característica de este maravilloso pais.

Quisiera extender mi más sincero agradecimiento a todos ellos, y muy en especial a un grupo de personas, las cuales contribuyeron de manera directa, aportando su valioso tiempo y compartiendo sus conocimientos, facilitando nuestras investigaciones y haciendo tan placentera nuestra esdadía.

Mi profunda gratitud al Sr. Alejandro Ponce Noboa, Presidente de Galatours en Guayaquil, por su contínua hospitalidad tanto en Guyaquil, como abordo del M/V BUCANERO, y por su gran apoyo sin el cual este libro no hubiese sido posible.

A Doris Welsh de Galapagos Center, por habernos proporcionado la más completa informacion pertinente a las mas recientes investigaciones efectuadas en las Islas Galápagos, y quien además fue responsable de todos los pormenores de los arreglos de nuestro viaje.

A el Capitán Juan Angel Cevallos, y a la tripulación entera del M/V BUCANERO, y muy en especial al Primer Oficial Rolando Garcia Pazmiño, y Segundo Oficial Nelson Crespo, nuestra gratitud por su inagotable paciencia al responder a nuestras interminables preguntas acerca del mar y de las islas.

A Luis Die, el guía naturalista abordo del M/V BUCANERO, por sus detalladas explicaciones concernientes a la extensa variedad de flora y fauna a lo largo de nuestro recorrido por las Islas Galápagos.

A nuestros compañeros de viaje, sobre todo A Jean Welsh, por su infallable sentido del humor y excelente compañía, y a Maria Gross, del Instituto Oceanográfico Internacional de Miami, por compartir tan generosamente sus conocimientos sobre el mar y la extensa variedad de las especies marinas y terrestres.

Y a Julie Rogers, renombrada fotógrafa profesional y extraordinaria compañera de viaje, por su excelente e inagotable labor que combinada con su gran sentido del humor, hicieran de esta invalorable experiencia, una aventura inolvidable!

Barbara Radcliffe Rogers

CONTENTS

I N T R O D U C T I O N

There is an atmosphere about the Galapagos unlike that of any other place in the world, an unmistakable primeval quality. It is as though we stand on its shores suddenly in the midst of another age, transported back millions of years to a landscape newly risen from the center of the earth. In this dramatic, barren land, too young to have eroded and too arid to have developed a deep soil cover, the swirling rush of lava is still fresh, its fluid lines visible everywhere.

The wild creatures, equally primeval, exist almost without fear of humans. They live amid the lava swirls and the coral beaches and in the bowls of the great craters. No great forests find a foothold here. Only the mangrove can find a place for its tangled

mass of roots in the tidal shoreline, and the Scalesia (sunflower tree) grows as a stunted shrub except in the humid zones of the higher islands. The palo santos trees are leafless through the long dry season, their gray trunks and white, twisted branches like bleached skeletons amid the prickly pear and thornbush. The rest is sedge and fern and saltbush and lichens.

It is a forbidding place with few safe anchorages, surrounded by treacherous currents, parched and sunbaked. Alone in a vast stretch of the Pacific Ocean, it has almost no drinking water, reminiscent of the desperate lines from The Rime of the Ancient Mariner, *"Water, water everywhere, but nary a drop to drink."*

Thirsty sailors put in there, searched its rocks for water, and left more thirsty than when they arrived. A canteen is still essential gear for anyone who ventures ashore.

Why then does this inhospitable, forbidding place attract a steady flow of visitors? It is surely not for the beaches (there are few), the resorts (there are none), the climate (cool seven months of the year; extremely hot during the other five), or the lush tropical scenery (there is none). It is only our insatiable curiosity about the earth we inhabit, the thirst for knowledge of what is past and what is beyond. Certainly no place on earth offers the scientist a better laboratory or the visitor a better view of the earth's beginnings.

It is an anomaly, too, a set of tropical islands without native palm trees, with penguins living astride the equator, fur seals sliding over coral beaches. Nowhere else in the world live large, seagoing lizards (marine iguanas) or cormorants that cannot fly, or finches that pry their food out of plants using a thorn as a tool.

Charles Darwin, whose name is associated with these islands more than any other, observed in his diary after only two weeks there the phenomenon that has compelled the curious—both scientist and layman—to visit the Galapagos: "Both in space and time, we seem to be brought somewhat near to that great fact—that mystery of mysteries—the first appearance of new beings on this earth...."

The rocky landscapes of the Galapagos have changed very little since the islands' formation.

On Santiago Island
(right) and North
Plaza (above), the
flow of molten lava
seems to have cooled
just yesterday, its
swirling shapes super-
imposed on a base of
cinder stones.

The Galapagos are new in geological terms, some scarcely one million years old, the oldest perhaps five million. Because of the islands' relative youth and the scarcity of plant life, it is possible to imagine these great cones of rock rising, hissing and boiling, out of the sea. In certain places, more recent lava flows seem to have cooled just yesterday, and steam still escapes from fumeroles.

The Galapagos began with a rush of acutely hot lava being forced through the earth's crust deep beneath the sea. Over millions of years these eruptions continued, each adding a layer of volcanic rock that was hardened by cold water, until at last an explosion of this molten magma broke the surface of the Pacific and the Galapagos became islands.

To understand the forces of vulcanism and how they have altered the face of the earth, we must look to the relatively new concept of plate tectonics, a theory which changed scientific thinking in the 1960s. Most volcanos are located along the edges of the gigantic floating, moving plates that encrust the surface of the earth. But the Galapagos are over 600 miles from the nearest margin volcanoes of the Andes and the same distance from the East Pacific Rift.

The corollary theory of "hot spots" suggests that volcanoes which lie so far from the edges of plates are caused by areas of hot magma beneath the plates that burst through as the plate shifts. The Hawaiian Islands show the same pattern of development, with older islands to one side of the group and active volcanoes on the other, showing the continued movement of the plates. This theory of hot spots, now widely accepted, explains as well the sloping pattern of the underwater platform from which the islands rise.

Determining the age of the Galapagos has been a long-term geological project. A number of obstacles have stood in the way. The most obvious of these is that volcanoes cover their origins with successive layers of nearly impermeable rock. Each new lava flow buries the earlier ones. Since the arid climate of the islands slows the formation of soil, which in turn prevents the growth of deep-rooted plants that break down the rock, erosion is minimal. Unlike most environments, the older rock here is simply not available for study.

> Another feature in these isles is their emphatic uninhabitableness...the Encantadas refuse to harbor even the outcasts of the beasts. Man and wolf alike disown them. Little but reptile life is here found; tortoises, lizards...No voice, no low, no howl is heard; the chief sound of life here is a hiss."
>
> Herman Melville, aboard the whaler Acushnet, *recorded later in* Las Encantadas

Radioisotope dating of those rock samples that are available is made difficult by the relative absence of potassium, in which radioactive decay is measured to determine age. Where radioisotope dating fails, or to corroborate it as evidence, a method called paleomagnetic stratigraphy is used. This dating method is based on the fact that the earth's magnetic pole has not always been in the north. In the time since the Galapagos were thrust from the sea, there have been two periods during which the pole has shifted to the south. Between these was a period of about a million years when the magnetic center was in the north, as it is now. By studying the iron-containing minerals in the lava flows, geologists can see in which direction they were pulled while the lava was still hot and fluid, thus determining the ages of the different flows.

The problem, of course, is that there has been more than one period in each direction within the lifetimes of the oldest islands. The additional physical evidence—vegetation, erosion, and radiocarbon dating—which is valuable in solving this problem elsewhere, is of limited use in Galapagos. The study is further complicated by the fact that some of the stone tested may have been formed in the ten or so million years

Espanola's profile clearly shows its origins as a slab of lava rock thrust up from beneath the sea. Although it lacks the dramatic cones that mark other islands, it is rich in wildlife.

of volcanic eruptions underwater, then thrust to the surface and held there by subsequent eruptions.

However, by painstaking research using each available method and comparison of the findings, geologists have established the age of the oldest islands to be at least 3.3 million years and perhaps as old as 5 million. Fossil evidence of life there dates from the last 2 million years. This makes the Galapagos considerably younger than other still-active volcanic island groups such as the Canary Islands or the Azores.

The more recent geology of the islands is equally difficult to study, but the sedimentary record left in the lake bed of El Junco's crater supplies stratas of plant evidence. These show that the crater has held lakes for two separate prolonged periods, broken by the Ice Age. Spores of water fern, although of different species, are present in two different layers of bottom mud, separated by a clay layer that holds no evidence of water plants. The modern lake is at least 10,000 years old, and the dry period appears to have lasted about 30,000 years.

There have been numerous other theories about the origins of the Galapagos, many of them put forth in response to the puzzling question of how animal and plant species first reached the archipelago. The simplest explanation, and one with corollary evidence elsewhere, is that the islands were once attached by a land bridge or at least by an ocean ridge dotted with islands (much like the Aleutians) that provided stepping stones for flora and fauna to spread from the mainland. Proponents of this theory point out that the islands are close enough to either Ecuador—600 miles (960 km)

The lava cactus (above), a common sight in the Galapagos, is nevertheless rarely found in bloom, as it is seen here on Fernandina Island. More recent geologic action has caused cracks and fissures in the swirled lava surface such as this one on Santiago Island (opposite page).

east—or Central America—1000 miles (1600 km) northeast—and there are submarine ridges connecting the Galapagos to each. The most likely of these would have been the Cocos Ridge, which reaches from Costa Rica almost to the Galapagos, although the Carnegie Ridge is only slightly lower and runs almost due east to Ecuador.

One variation on the theory suggests that the Cocos Ridge was, until 12 million years ago, a peninsula stretching to within 100 miles (160 km) of a much larger land mass of which the Galapagos are the only remaining summits. This theory is consistent with the similarities found between some of the Galapagos species and those of Central America.

The distribution of many of the same plants and animals among the central islands has been offered as evidence to support the theory of a larger land mass containing at least the three central islands. However, the similarities can also be explained by the fact that the ocean levels were known to have dropped significantly during the Ice Age, which would have made travel between these islands possible, either entirely by land or in a much shorter distance by water.

One stepping-stone theory suggests that the volcanic action proceeded from the continent, and that earlier links in the chain, being much older, have eroded away. Although deep-sea research and soundings in the area have not been sufficient to either prove or disprove the theory, there is no evidence to date of these worn-down volcanic cones. There is also no geological evidence that there was ever any larger land mass connecting the islands with each other.

Darwin was astonished at the variations in the wildlife between the different islands and observed that "the profound depth of the ocean between the islands and their apparently recent (in a geological sense) volcanic origins, render it highly unlikely that they were ever connected."

A hundred and fifty years later, after intense study using more recently developed methods, geologists agree with his observations, just as they generally agree that the islands are not only oceanic in origin, but have always been entirely separate from the continent.

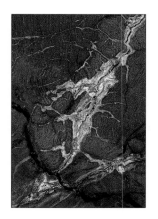

Mineral formations, along with the varied patterns and forms of lava flow, give Santiago some of the most interesting surface geology.

The distinctive surface patterns of the pahoehoe (right), or ropy lava, can be clearly seen in Santiago Island.

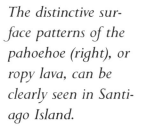

Lava tubes (left) were formed as rivers of molten lava cooled and hardened on the top while still flowing under the surface. Few of the upthrusts of lava crust are as dramatic as that of Pinnacle Rock (opposite page).

It was the hope of finding water, not the forbidding coastal landscapes, that enticed early mariners to come ashore. The last bird one would expect to find living astride the equator is the penguin (opposite page), whose origins and habits are clearly Arctic.

THE · DISCOVERY

The islands had the better part of 2 to 5 million years for species to arrive and for the process of evolution to alter them before man ever set foot there. Unlike most places (the volcanic islands of Madeira are another exception), the Galapagos had no aboriginal population, and the first record of human presence dates from approximately the fifteenth century.

Although there is no contemporaneous written record of pre-conquest Peru, there was a strong tradition of oral history using systems of knotted cords that signified ancient chants and stories recalling the history of the Inca people. In the early years of the Spanish conquest, the historian Sarmiento de Gamba spent years collecting these stories and the personal accounts of people who could remember events of importance. When he had recorded many of

these tales, he called the local historians together to check and approve his chronicle, *History of the Incas*. Fourteen years later, Cabello de Balboa wrote *History of Peru*, also based on the oral traditions of the local peoples.

Both these historians record the story of the tenth king of the Incas, Tupac Yupanqui, grandfather of Atahualpa, last king of the Incas. Having heard stories from the traders who put their balsa-wood rafts in along the coast of two islands to the west where there was gold, the Inca king moved his armies to the great balsa forests near what is now Guayaquil, Ecuador.

There they built a fleet of rafts, fitted with sails, and with 20,000 men set out to find the islands. They returned, from nine months to a year later, with "some black men, much gold, a chair made of brass, and the skin and jawbone of a horse." He named the islands he saw "the Island of Fire" and "the Outside Island."

Allowing for the fact that he also stopped for a coastal raid on the way back, which might have been the source of most of the strange group of trophies—none of which, certainly, came from the Galapagos—the rest of the story is quite possible. Potsherds and other pre-Spanish Conquest artifacts have been found in the Galapagos, demonstrating that indigenous South American seafarers at least visited the islands in the century before the Spaniards arrived. Also, we now know from Thor Heyerdahl's expeditions that balsa rafts with centerboards, an ancient Peruvian and Ecuadorian style of craft, can tack into the wind and are quite capable of sailing as far as 600 miles (960 km) and returning. For most of the year, the Humboldt Current sweeps everything that puts to sea along the coast of Peru in a long, curving course toward the Galapagos. A large number of rafts (although a number sufficient to carry 20,000 troops is likely an exaggeration) spread out in a wide formation would have trouble *not* coming upon the Galapagos. And since there are no volcanic islands anywhere else close by, the Island of Fire would have been an unusual traveler's tale to have invented.

While it is quite likely that Inca historians, in an effort to impress their new conquerors, may have embroidered the story a bit, adding to the size of the fleet and even to the booty brought home (they had reason to know that tales of gold brought a gleam to the Spaniards' eyes), it is unlikely that a totally invented story would have been so widely known and often told.

"We have already mentioned those Birds called Penguins to be about the bigness of Geese; but upon second thoughts to call them Fowls I think improper, because they have neither Feathers nor Wings, but only two Fins or Flaps, wherewith they are helped to swim.

Captain Woods Voyage Through the Streights of Magellan, 1669

More clearly documented is the accidental visit of Fray Tomas de Berlenga, bishop of Panama, in 1535, when his ship was caught in a calm and then currents swept it far from its planned course from Panama to Peru. Having drifted at sea for more than a week, the voyagers were desperate for water when they sighted the Galapagos. They planted the cross and the flag and spent another week searching for water. They eventually found enough in the hollows of rocks to replenish their supplies, but only barely, and not in time to avoid some loss of both men and horses.

The Bishop wrote at length to King Charles V of Spain, and his letter gives us the first description of the Galapagos.

> Once out, they found nothing but seals and turtles and such big tortoises that each could carry a man on top of itself, and many iguanas that are like serpents. On another day we saw another island, larger than the first, and with great sierras [mountains]....
>
> On this second one, the same conditions prevailed as on the first; many seals, turtles, iguanas, tortoises, many birds like those of Spain, but so silly they do not know how to flee...on the whole island I do not think that there is a place where one might sow a bushel of corn, because most of it is full of very big stones; so much so, that it seems as though sometime God had showered stones.

As later mariners, also arriving thirsty, were to discover, the fleshy leaves of the prickly pear offered juice. "...with the thirst the people felt, they resorted to a leaf of some thistles like prickly pears, and because they were somewhat juicy, although not very tasty, we began to eat of them and squeeze them to draw all the water out of them, and then drank it as if it were rosewater."

Although Fray Tomas evidently didn't consider the islands important enough to name, and his letter remained almost untouched in the Spanish archives for three centuries, a Flemish cartographer heard of the discovery from the ship's pilot and word of the bishop's letter. In 1574, the islands first appeared on a map, Abraham Ortelius's "Orbis Terrarum," where they were named Islas de Galapagos, islands of tortoises, from Fray Tomas's account.

The bishop had been sent to Peru by the king of Spain to settle the bitter disputes among the conquistadors and to admonish them to moderate their ruthless treatment of the native population. His visit had little effect upon either situation, and in 1546, after trying to defend a more humane course in the face of the bloodthirsty policies of Pizarro's commander, Carvajal, Diego Centeno was driven from Peru. He sent one of his officers, Diego de Rivadeneira, to sail north, but he was threatened by Carvajal's men wherever he tried to land.

Turning east into the open sea, by then almost without provisions, Rivadeneira eventually sighted islands that he described as seeming to be perpetually covered with cloud, and some having smoke rising from them. They had fled without compass or pilot, so they had no idea of their bearings, but their description of turtles, sea lions, and iguanas leaves little doubt that they had rediscovered the Galapagos. Like so many others who would arrive thirsty after them, they left without finding water.

A variety of other early sailors left fragments of mention, usually calling the islands by the seamen's name, Las Encantadas—the bewitched. To ships drifting becalmed, the islands seemed to recede and appear again mysteriously and to drift somewhere above the surface of the sea. In addition, navigation was largely guesswork in the late sixteenth century, and the strong currents played tricks. So ships sailed, they thought, directly to where they had previously seen islands and saw none.

North Wind Picture Archives

The endless action of the waves is one of the few eroding forces on the face of the Galapagos, since there is little rain to cause inland weathering (opposite page). The first views Europeans had of the Galapagos were in artists' engravings, some done from sketches by travelers, others made up from written descriptions.

Following page: The giant tortoises on Isabela Island spend much of their time in the pond inside the Alcedo crater.

The clear waters off the shore of Espanola Island are popular for swimmers, but sharp rocks protruding through the sand make land approach difficult.

BUCCANEERS · AND CASTAWAYS

Following the harassment of the native populations by the Spanish, it became the Spaniards' turn to be harassed by British and French buccaneers, who intercepted their ships full of treasure bound for Spain. These pirates and privateers had among them several highly articulate diarists, and from them we have the first detailed descriptions of the Galapagos and accounts of events there.

Buccaneers used the uninhabited islands as safe harbor, often storing their supplies and plunder there between raids. Of these, Ambrose Cowley made the first charts of the islands, which these buccaneers had come to know quite well. His chart remained far more reliable than one made a century later by the captain of the Spanish Armada. It was Cowley who gave the islands their English names.

Aboard the same ship, *The Batchelor's Delight* (as they had christened their newly captured Danish prize), was William Dampier, whose journal provides detailed botanical and zoological information as well as weather observations. Until the arrival of Darwin, Dampier's accounts stood as the most complete and reli-

able information on the Galapagos. His journal, which he carried wrapped in section of bamboo sealed with wax to prevent possible damage from the sea, ranks him with the great naturalist explorers.

> The guanos [iguanas] here are as fat and large as any I ever saw; they are so tame that a man may knock down twenty in an hour's time with a club. The land turtle here are so numerous that 500 or 600 men might subsist on them alone for several months, without any other sort of provision. They are extraordinarily large and fat, and so sweet that no pullet eats more pleasantly. One of the largest of these creatures will weigh one hundred and fifty to two hundred weight, and some of them are two feet or two feet six inches over the callapee or belly.

Dampier actually seems to have liked the Galapagos, as did Darwin after him, while to others they were at best a poor refuge and source of turtle meat. He frequently refers to the availability of water in places where others had searched fruitlessly, so it is evident that his visits occurred during a time of unusual rainfall. Perhaps this explains his reaction to their desolate shores, but it more likely stems from his interest and curiosity about the natural world there. He was no ordinary freebooter, and with the publication of his *New Voyage Round the World* he set a style for literary travel and adventure narrative that influenced Daniel Defoe, Jonathan Swift, and other writers since.

It was on Dampier's last voyage, now turned respectable and under commission from the Admiralty, that his ship, *The Dutchess*, rescued Alexander Selkirk, a seaman marooned for over four years on Juan Fernandez Island. Dampier had known Selkirk previously and urged his captain to make him an officer.

When, after laying siege to Guayaquil, they returned to the Galapagos, but were unable to find water in any of the places Dampier had remembered, it was Selkirk's experiences in finding sustenance on a desert island that provided guidance for them as they recovered from the fever most of the crew had contracted during the occupation.

Selkirk returned to England, wrote a long account of his four years as a castaway, and at the suggestion of a friend, showed it to the young Daniel Defoe for advice. Defoe is said to have kept the manuscript for a considerable time, and when he finally returned it, described it as useless and discouraged Selkirk from any hope of turning it into anything. Shortly after, Defoe's *Robinson Crusoe* was published, bringing fortune and prominence to Defoe and nothing to Selkirk.

Floreana (Charles) Island had a later castaway, an Irish seaman put ashore there in the early 1800s. His story comes to us from another offi-cer of scientific bent and literary skill. Captain David Porter of the U.S. Navy, who sailed in the area during the War of 1812, records that Patrick Watkins had left a British ship some years earlier and had been able to survive, living in a crude hut he had built and growing vegeta-bles that he exchanged for rum with passing ships. Porter records that he was "so wild and savage in his man-ner and appearance that he struck everyone with horror. For some years this wretched being lived by himself on this desolate spot without any apparent desire than that of pro-curing rum in suffic-ient quantities to keep himself intoxicated...."

Watkins later abduct-ed an American sea-man with the purpose of enslaving him, but the seaman overpowered him and escaped to his ship. Then Watkins began to abduct sailors by getting them drunk until their ships sailed with-out them; then he would make slaves of them. He eventually set out for the mainland with five of these hapless seamen in a stolen boat. He arrived in Guayaquil alone, and Porter could only surmise what had happened to the "slaves" as food and water grew short on the voyage.

> *I came to Anchor under in a good Bay having seaven fathom water, ther being upon this Island to the South end a good Harbor for many Shipps to ride, I beleive his Majestyes Navy might ride there in safety, we put the Boat a shoare, but found no water there but wee found Land Turtle very great, and Sea Turtle, very good and large and great plenty, and a sort of ffowles called fflemingo with Goanoes, which our men brought aboard, the small Birds being not in the least posessed with feare, they lighted on our mens heads and Armes and they tooke them off, which at first seemed strange to me...*
>
> —Captain Edward Davis, buccaneer, 1684

Giant tortoises are known to have once inhabited nearly all the Earth's conti-nents, but are now found only here and on the islands of the Indian Ocean.

THE · WHALERS

From about 1800 onward, whalers replaced the buccaneers and privateers in the waters around the Galapagos. Since the 1793 exploratory voyage of Captain James Colnett of the British navy had established that there was both anchorage and food available there, British whaling ships had become frequent visitors. Captain Colnett's trip, like so many others of the British navy, was a multipurpose one, intended to establish the feasibility of whaling there as well as to provide scientific data and charts. He kept notes of his observations and his eye for zoological and botanical detail was keen.

> I frequently observed the whales leave these islands and go to the Westward and in a few days return with augmented numbers. I have also seen the whales coming, as it were, from the main, and passing along from the dawn of day to the night in one extended line as if they were in haste to reach the Galapagoes.

Along with safe anchorage, the Galapagos provided an almost endless supply of meat from the giant tortoise. This welcome relief from salt pork and infested biscuits could not only be captured easily, but could be stored live, without water or food for up to a year, for use while whaling and on the voyage home. It is estimated that buccaneers, whalers and other seafarers removed 150,000 to 200,000 tortoises from the Galapagos in less than three centuries (1500 to 1800), thus decimating the populations of this gentle giant.

It is thought to be Colnett who established the islands' first post office, which still captures the imagination of travelers and is in use to this day. On the north shore of Charles Island (Floreana), a well-known anchorage of both buccaneers and whalers, stands a barrel affixed to a stump. After rounding Cape Horn on a voyage that might last four or five years, sailors left mail for their sponsors and families in the barrel, to be picked up and carried home by eastbound vessels.

Captain Porter of the U.S.S. *Essex* made good use of this mail service during the War of 1812, when he read the mail left there and was able to determine the location of a good number of the whaling ships. He soon captured three of them, replenishing his supplies from their holds, and converted two of them into warships. The whaling crews, given the option of being kept on board as prisoners, agreed to serve as hands. With several ships in his command, Porter had simply to cruise among the islands, waiting for whalers to put in, or go out into the whaling waters, where the slower vessels were no match for his man-of-war.

By the time his mission ended, he had so many ships in his fleet that he had run out of officers and had to put a twelve-year-old midshipman in charge of one vessel. It turned out that necessity forced a fortunate decision, for the boy was David Farragut, who later became the U.S. Navy's first full admiral.

All the while, Porter was busy making detailed scientific records of everything he saw. He carefully describes the giant tortoises in a day when they were plentiful, before their decimation at the hands of the whalers. He recognized the differences between the tortoises of different islands and suspected that the marine iguanas were a unique species: "From their taking to the water very readily we were induced to believe them a distinct species from those found in the West Indies." He evidently knew something, too, of geology, for he recognized the islands to be of fairly recent volcanic origin.

Along with scientific observation, his journal is filled with well-written accounts of the day-to-day life on the islands and the search for food and water. He was well versed enough in botany to recognize plants that could be put to use:

> We were enabled to procure here, also in large quantities, an herb much resembling spinach, and so called by our people; likewise, various other pot-herbs and prickly pears in great abundance, which were not only of an excellent flavour, but a sovereign anti-scorbutic as well. It afforded me great pleasure to observe that they were so much relished by our people. The cotton plant was found growing spontaneously....

The Post Office Barrel on Floreana has been in use since the days when whaling ships put it there. One of the few safe harbors among the islands, the harbor soon became known as P.O. Bay.

... our ears were suddenly assailed by a sound that could only be equaled by ten thousand thunders bursting upon the air at once; while at the same instant, the whole hemisphere was lighted up with a horrid glare that might have appalled the stoutest heart! I soon ascertained that one of the volcanoes of Narborough Island, which had quietly slept for the past ten years, had suddenly broken forth with accumulated vengeance. ... The heavens appeared to be one blaze of fire, intermingled with millions of falling stars and meteors; while the flames shot upward from the peak of Narborough to the height of at least two thousand feet in the air. ... A river of melted lava was now seen rushing down the side of the mountain, persuing a serpentine course to the sea, a distance of about three miles from the blazing orifice of the volcano. The dazzling stream descended in a gully, one-fourth of a mile in width, persenting the appearance of a tremendous torrent of melted iron running from the furnace. ... At three A.M. I ascertained the temperature of the water... to be 61° [F], while that of the air was 71°. At eleven A.M. the air was 113° and the water 100°, the eruption still continuing with unabated fury. The Tartar's anchorage was about ten miles to the northward of the mountain, and the heat was so great that the melted pitch was running from the vessel's seams and the tar dropping from the rigging. ... The murcury continued to rise until four P.M., when the temperature of the air had increased to 123° and that of the water to 105°.

Captain Benjamin Morrell of the Tartar, 1825

MURDER
· A N D ·
DISAPPEARANCE

It is curious that in an era of colonial zeal, when land was constantly being claimed for one crown or another, that Spanish, Ecuadorian, British, and American ships had all visited and used the Galapagos without any of them laying claim. It is true that the bishop of Panama planted a flag there, but Spain made no territorial claim to the islands. It wasn't until 1831, after Ecuador had been freed from Spain and had broken her confederation with Colombia and become independent, that a Colonel Hernandez took possession of the Galapagos in the name of Ecuador.

General Jose Villamil formed a company for the colonization of Charles Island, taking with him eighty soliders who had been condemned for their part in a rebellion. The population grew over the next few years to two or three hundred settlers, who cultivated croplands in the higher moist zone and hunted wild goats (which had multiplied at a phenomenal rate since a few had escaped from the *Essex* while they were pastured ashore).

The purpose of the colony had been to develop the orchilla moss industry. This moss, which was used for a dye, grew on some of the islands, and Villamil had hoped to gather and export it. But the plan never worked well and the settlers' chief source of income became the supplying of food to the whaling ships that put in at Charles Island.

Ecuador began to use the settlement as a penal colony, and after five years, Villamil left. He was replaced by Colonel Jose Williams, whose iron-fisted command was enforced by a pack of dogs that accompanied him everywhere. His style of keeping order finally led to a mutiny. Williams escaped, and when Villamil returned to assess the damage, he found only a few settlers left on Charles. Most had dispersed to other islands, partly because of Williams and partly due to the extinction of the Charles turtle population, which had been their major source of food.

Villamil moved what little was left of his settlement to Chatham (San Cristobal) Island, where he had hoped to mine coal. (One wonders what led him to believe that coal was there or how he expected to mine it from the impervious lava.) In 1851 a group of convicts ambushed the crew of the American whaler *George Howland* while they were ashore on Charles looking for water. They forced the remaining crew to return to Chatham, where they murdered the commander of the colony. After outfitting the ship from the island's supplies, the convicts set out for a life of piracy under the leadership of one of their own named Briones.

He had somehow gotten word of a coup d'état planned by General Juan Jose Flores, a former president of Ecuador then in exile in Peru. Briones planned to intercept Flores's fleet, thwart the coup, and be hailed as a hero in Guayaquil before retiring with his freedom and his booty. He did indeed intercept the lead ship of the fleet, killed its crew, and sailed into Guayaquil as planned. But Guayaquil's people had seen enough of pirates, and instead of a pardon, they hanged the lot of them.

This incident, which involved the seizure of an American ship, brought the Galapagos to the attention of the United States. Although there were those who felt that the U.S. should acquire the islands, since its whalers were the main users of the Galapagos economically, and Ecuador seemed to have little interest in either governing or securing the Galapagos, the idea never really caught on.

Instead, Villamil, still trying to find a resource to exploit, convinced Americans involved in the guano trade with Peru that the Galapagos were an untapped guano mine. The U.S. signed a treaty, loaning Ecuador $3 million in exchange for guano rights, and promised to recognize Ecuador as the owner of the Galapagos. But like many of Villamil's other schemes, this one was based on a false premise and poor investigation. There were no guano deposits and the agreement was never ratified.

The whole affair focused international attention on the Galapagos, and although the islands were of no particular use to any of the major powers, neither Napoleon III nor England wanted the United States to have special privileges there. The British remembered from the

Lava "ovens" like this one on Santiago are another of the unusual geological features left by millennia of volcanic eruption.

Island sunsets in the Galapagos are unfailingly beautiful, but last only a matter of minutes. Because of the equatorial latitude, the sun drops straight below the horizon without the twilight of temperate and arctic latitudes.

War of 1812 what a nuisance an enemy presence there could be to Pacific shipping. However, since no country really wanted them as long as they were not about to fall into the hands of another major power, all were content to let Ecuador keep them. Quito had enough of its own problems and was certainly not a threatening presence there.

There followed another attempt to exploit the orchilla moss by reopening Villamil's abandoned settlement on Charles Island, but it, too, collapsed in violence after a mutiny and the murders of its captain and several others.

Ten years later, Manuel Cobos tried again with the establishment of the El Progresso settlement on Chatham. Once again, using convict laborers, he built a sugarcane plantation

and fruit and vegetable farm that flourished for a time. But the total lack of government authority and control there allowed Cobos to establish a slave-labor system. Workers were paid with credit to Cobos-owned stores, and no one could leave because the boats were his, too.

Those abuses continued until 1904, when Cobos was murdered and the remainder of the group returned to Guayaquil in one of his ships. At their trial, the story of Cobos's oppression came out and ships were dispatched to rescue the people he had abandoned alone on other uninhabited islands as punishment. One had survived for three years on Santa Cruz, but only remains were found of another on James.

Other colonization attempts followed, each ending in failure. Meanwhile the islands continued to claim ships that, becalmed and caught like Fray Thomas in the Humboldt Current, were swept to the Galapagos, their passengers hungry and thirsty. A Norwegian ship wrecked there in 1906, and its survivors kept themselves alive for months with no water except that which could be gleaned from cactus leaves.

Around the turn of the century, several foreign powers became interested in the Galapagos as the potential site of a coaling station where they could refuel ships. France and the United States vied for rights or outright ownership. Chile also expressed an interest. Ecuador itself, which until then had only a passing interest in the islands, began to see their value with the opening of the Panama Canal.

Ecuador did not wish the Galapagos to fall into foreign hands. Yet they couldn't defend the islands themselves and were afraid of losing them unless they granted rights to a nation that could. President Elroy Alfaro summed up his country's position quite succinctly when he said, "For us, the archipelago is a distant hope, but an immediate danger."

During this time, other settlers came and went. One group made a subsistence living by exporting sulfur from the crater on Southern Albermarle (Isabela) Island. The most notorious of these settlements was certainly in keeping with the islands' history of violence.

In 1929 a German doctor and self-styled philosopher, Friedrich Ritter, and a former patient, Dore Strauch, arrived at the Galapagos intending to prove the doctor's rather peculiar theories on Nietzsche's Superman. He had lured Dore into his dream of a Utopia on a paradise island where they would live in harmony with nature. Frau Strauch had been so concerned to leave things neatly resolved at home that she even arranged a match between her husband and Ritter's long-suffering wife!

Shortly after the Ritters had carved their farm out of the highland forest on Charles Island, a determined German couple with a nearly blind son arrived. The Witmers were not welcomed by the Ritters, and the women in particular took an instant mutual dislike. They lived their largely separate lives until the arrival of a "baroness" who, with her male harem, intended to turn the island into a resort for the wealthy yachtsmen who were beginning to stop regularly at the Galapagos.

In the course of their long mutual habitation of the same island, the only thing that Dore Strauch and Frau Witmer agreed on was their hatred of Baroness Wagner. The men in her retinue changed with regular departures and arrivals, and her former favorite, Lorenz, became an ill-used lackey, who, when he finally escaped, took refuge with the Witmers. Dr. Ritter and Frau Strauch had in the meantime become estranged.

The sudden disappearance of the baroness and her current favorite, the equally sudden death of Dr. Ritter by food poisoning, and the discovery of Lorenz's body, mummified by the sun, on another island, wove a murder mystery that has never been solved. The plot was further confused by the erratic and unexplained behavior of nearly everyone concerned. Both Dore Strauch, who left Floreana, and Frau Witmer, who stayed, wrote books about the incident, which had provided both the German and American press with fodder for some time.

John Treherne, a British zoologist who came to do research on the Galapagos, heard the story and wrote a thorough account of the events entitled *The Galapagos Affair*, which reads as well as any fictional murder mystery.

The islands had been of no strategic importance in World War I, but with the rise of Japanese power in the Pacific and the increased activity of Japanese fishing boats in the area, the

United States began to watch them more closely. In order to prevent any serious threats to Panama Canal shipping, the United States Navy began a series of exercises there, and President Roosevelt visited the islands aboard a Navy ship in 1938. After the attack on Pearl Harbor, Ecuador quickly gave the United States the right to build a base on South Seymour Island.

In 1942 the island became what American sailors called "the rock"—an airstrip, water distillation plant, repair and refueling station, and constant guard over the Pacific entrance to the Panama Canal. In 1947, the Navy turned the base over to Ecuador, and local settlers were welcome to use its buildings as materials for their homes. Now called Baltra, South Seymour Island is still the gateway to those arriving by air.

While modern short-trip visitors find the variety of seascapes beautiful, their monotony quickly wore on American sailors stationed there during WW II.

Bartolome (above) is a small island with virtually no plant or animal life, but is visited for its fascinating geology and the fine views from its summit.
The origins of the land iguana (right) are among the many mysteries of evolution.

CHAPTER · TWO
THE · ISLANDS · TODAY

What does the modern-day visitor find on the islands beside the ghosts of their bloody past? Apart from Santa Cruz Island, where the Darwin Research Station and a few tourist facilities and stores form the little town of Puerto Ayora, in Academy Bay, and a similar settlement at Puerto Boquerizo Moreno on Chatham (San Cristobal) Island, the islands are still sparsely inhabited.

European settlers began to arrive after World War II, and Ecuador has encouraged its own people to colonize the Galapagos. San Cristobal is the administrative capital, and has an Ecuadorian naval station. By the mid 1980s the population of the islands had grown to approximately 10,000 permanent residents, most of whom live on Santa Cruz and San Cristobal. The population is currently increasing at a rate of twelve to fifteen percent a year, a huge growth rate by any standard, mostly due to the arrival of new Educadorian settlers hoping to

profit from the boom in tourism. Farming has succeeded on Santa Cruz, San Cristobal, and Isabela, where there is moisture on the higher slopes of the volcanic cones. Cattle raised there are exported to the mainland, along with coffee and fish. Of the total land area of the islands, 97 percent has been designated a national park, excluding only the settled areas on those three islands and Floreana, plus all of Baltra, which is now an air and naval base.

Except for the settlements and farms and Baltra's airstrip, the islands look much as they did when the early sailors saw them. Iguanas and lizards sun on the parched rocks, birds nest there, and the volcanoes still put on an occasional show. Apart from the visitors, whose numbers and routes are controlled, the land still belongs largely to the wildlife that has brought the islands to the attention of the scientific world, at least ever since Darwin first arrived there on the H.M.S. *Beagle*.

Although Charles Darwin wrote one of the world's greatest travel chronicles, he never again left England after the single voyage of his youth.

DARWIN:
THIRTY-FIVE · DAYS
THAT · SPARKED
A · REVOLUTION

Charles Darwin was not an eminent scientist when he boarded the *Beagle*. He was, in fact, a mediocre student who, having narrowly achieved his degree at Cambridge, was about to become a country clergyman at the instigation of his father. His position as naturalist for the *Beagle*'s voyage was brought about by a series of slim coincidences.

Darwin was the son of a well-respected Shropshire doctor, raised in England's cultured middle class. His grandfather was the indepen-

dent-thinking philosopher Erasmus Darwin, who had espoused the notion of the natural "improvement" and descent of many species from a common ancestor, views that were as heretical in pre-Victorian England as those of his grandson were to be two generations later. Darwin's uncle was Josiah Wedgwood, famed for the manufacture of fine pottery. Like the Darwins, the Wedgwoods were well-educated freethinkers.

Although Charles Darwin noted in his autobiography that his father and teachers had agreed that he was "a very ordinary boy, rather below the common standard in intellect," he did grow up in an environment where independent thinking was highly prized. He notes, too, that he was a collector from his childhood days—

plants, shells, insects, minerals—whatever specimens of nature he could acquire. Indeed, at Cambridge he took more interest in his beetle collection than in his classes.

He was fortunate to live in a day when acceptance at a good university did not depend on academic record. He studied medicine briefly and without interest at Edinburgh, and learned little at Cambridge, but it was at Cambridge that he met the friends and professors who encouraged his natural interest in science.

Because Darwin never took himself very seriously, he never expected that he would be able to make much of his life and so did not consider a career in a field so exacting as science. He agreed with his father that the life of a country clergyman would be about the best he could do; that was an occupation well suited to someone who enjoyed the study of nature.

Professor John Stevens Henslow, chairman of the department of botany at Cambridge University, saw more potential for Darwin, whose curiosity and methodical approach impressed him. Henslow encouraged him to study geology and arranged for him to work with the respected geologist Adam Sedgewick. From the latter Darwin acquired some knowledge of geology, but also learned a curious thing about scientists of that era.

He tells in his autobiography of showing Sedgewick a large, worn volute shell that a workman had found in a gravel pit. Sedgewick said that it must have been thrown there, because there was no geological reason for it to be there. Darwin accepted this, but was astonished when Sedgewick went on to say that if it had really been embedded there, "it would be the greatest misfortune to geology as it would overthrow all we know about the superficial deposits of the Midland counties." Darwin could not understand that a man of science would not be delighted and fascinated by a new piece of evidence or an unusual phenomenon

simply because it did not fit into an accepted grouping of facts.

On his return from the trip with Sedgewick, Darwin found a letter from Henslow telling him about the position on the *Beagle* for which Henslow had recommended him. The purpose of the voyage was to continue charting the South American coast and fix the exact longitudes for the navy. Captain Fitzroy would share his cabin with a young man who would be willing to go on this two-year voyage as a naturalist without pay. Darwin was anxious to accept, but his father thought the idea foolish and refused to give his permission, so Darwin turned down the offer. Fortunately, his uncle, Josiah Wedgewood, intervened and persuaded Dr. Darwin to consent.

Darwin's interest in the trip was prompted in great part by his recent reading of Baron Alexander von Humboldt's *A Personal Narrative of Travels to the Equinoctial Regions of America During the Years of 1790–1804.* This glimpse of the natural world of the tropics had fired his imagination and he later said that Humboldt's book and *Introduction to the Study of Natural Philoso-*

An early artist's rendition of the Beagle *visiting the Galapagos.*

phy by Sir J. Hirschel, "stirred up in me a burning zeal to add even the most humble contribution to the noble structure of Natural Science. No one or a dozen other books influenced me nearly so much as these two."

Captain Robert Fitzroy, a deeply religious man of twenty-six, had his own reasons for wanting a naturalist on his expedition, and although Darwin's background was far different from his own, he felt that an amateur naturalist headed for a clergyman's life would suit his purposes well. Fitzroy wanted to find the scientific proof, which the naturalist's eye would surely discover, to support the currently popular literal translation of the Book of Genesis.

His naturalist would, he hoped, find in his exploration evidence of the flood and of the creation of each creature on earth in its exact present form. Darwin at this stage in his life also believed this, as did most people of strict Victorian upbringing. He questioned neither the fact nor the relevance of biblical teachings and did not view the story of the creation as allegorical.

From the beginning of the voyage—a very rough one—Darwin was violently seasick, but as soon as they reached their first stop in the Cape Verde Islands, off the coast of Africa, Darwin was quickly at work observing every detail and collecting specimens, "hearing the notes of unknown birds and seeing new insects fluttering about still newer flowers." The ship's next major stop was Rio de Janeiro, where Darwin first encountered the paradise of a tropical rain forest.

Unlike the vast majority of visitors before him, Darwin found the Sesuvium-covered barren landscapes of the Galapagos as fascinating as its unusual inhabitants.

He wrote to Henslow that he was afraid that his lack of formal scientific training would hinder him and feared that he would not bring back the right specimens. Although he didn't realize it then, it may have been his lack of formal studies that left his mind and imagination free enough to observe what was there, not what fitted the accepted theories.

At that time people believed that the world had been populated on several occasions in its history and that each period had ended in a cataclysm after which God had created new species. This theory accounted for, and was considered proven by, the different stratas of fossils, each group of which in any location was different. Each species was created in the exact form in which it would remain and went from generation to generation, with each child exactly like its parents.

In Bahia Blanca, Darwin found his first evidence that this might not be so. On a beach there he "found the head of some large animal stuck in a soft rock. It took me nearly three hours to get it out. As far as I am able to judge, it is allied to the rhinocerous." Later he found a huge fossilized jawbone containing one tooth from a rodent the size of an elephant and related to the sloth.

Darwin noted that it was very curious that God had placed these ancient giant toxodons in the same place as the much smaller, but similar, capybaras and sloths live today. He didn't have answers, but he was already asking the questions. When he showed the fossils to Fitzroy, the captain said they were two creatures who hadn't made it to the ark in time.

Although he had no idea how or why, Darwin was already beginning to wonder if the animals he saw alive in the pampas and rain forests could perhaps be descendants of ancient beasts greatly altered by time. When he reached the Galapagos, he began to fill in the gaps and formulate what became his later theories.

One senses in reading Darwin's diaries the excitement he felt when the *Beagle* landed in each new port and Darwin, pockets bulging with notebooks and collecting apparatus, eagerly waited to go ashore. He was not as enchanted with the beauty of the Galapagos as he had been on first standing in a rain forest.

Nothing could be less inviting than the first appearance. A broken field of black basaltic lava, thrown into the most rugged waves, and crossed by great fissures, is everywhere covered by stunted, sun-burnt brushwood, which shows little signs of life. The dry and parched surface, being heated by the noonday sun, gave to the air a close and sultry feeling, like that from a stove; we fancied even that the bushes smelt unpleasantly.

As he had done elsewhere, Darwin examined every detail of the island, collecting specimens and making copious notes on everything he saw and was told. His notes on the tortoise detailed its travel to find water, its drinking habits, the noises of the mating season, the vulnerability of newly hatched young, how the old die, even a measured record of its rate of travel.

The tortoises, when purposely moving towards any point, travel by night and day, and arrive at their journey's end much sooner than would be expected. The inhabitants, from observing marked individuals, consider that they travel a distance of about eight miles in two or three days. One large tortoise which I watched walked at the rate of sixty yards in ten minutes, that is 360 yards in the hour, or four miles a day—allowing a little time for it to eat on the road.

Charles Darwin's notes and diaries were meticulous in detail, even to measuring the speed of the tortoise.

He describes climbing on board these giants, rapping smartly on the rear of the carapace and being borne off, trying to keep his balance on the lurching round form. The picture of Darwin, or any other man of great reputation, jogging along the lava on a tortoise seems preposterous. But such strange things happen routinely on these islands that the ludicrous image of Darwin riding tortoise-back seems less odd in their context.

Darwin was both an observer and a reporter; no detail was too small to mention. He listened to every local account and added the observations of those who lived there to his own notes. It was Vice-Governor Larson who pointed out the sometimes subtle differences between the tortoises of different islands, saying that he could quickly tell which island any had come from. Darwin pondered the reasons for this in his diary.

I never dreamed that islands about fifty or sixty miles [80 or 100 km] apart, and most of them in sight of each other, formed of precisely the same rocks, placed under a quite similar climate, rising to a nearly equal height, would have been differently tenanted. . . .

The distribution of the tenants of this archipelago would not be nearly so wonderful, if, for instance, one island had a mocking-thrush and a second island some other quite distinct genus; if one island had its genus of lizard, and a second island another distinct genus, or none whatever; or if the different islands were inhabited, not by representative species of the same genera of plants, but by totally different genera, as does to a certain extent hold good. . . . But it is the circumstance that several of the islands possess their own species of the tortoise, mocking-thrush, finches, and numerous plants, these species having the same general habits, occupying analogous situations, and obviously filling the same place in the natural economy of this archipelago, that strikes me with wonder. It may be suspected that some of these representative species . . . may hereafter prove to be only well-marked races, but this would be of equally great interest. . . .

The only light I can throw on this remarkable difference in the inhabitants of the different islands is that very strong currents of the sea running in a westerly and west-north-west direction must separate, as far as transportal by the sea is concerned, the southern islands from the northern ones. . . . As the archipelago is free to a most remarkable degree from gales of wind, neither the birds, insects, nor lighter seeds would be blown from island to island.

He was a participant as well as an observer, and experimented with the creatures in order to learn more about their habits. He tells of throwing a marine iguana into the sea:

The nature of the lizard's food, as well as the structure of its tail and feet, and the fact of its having been seen voluntarily swimming out at sea absolutely prove its aquatic habits; yet there is in this respect one strange anomaly, namely that when frightened it will not enter the water. . . . I threw one several times as far as I could into a deep pool left by the retiring tide, but it invariably returned in a direct line to the spot where I stood. . . . Perhaps this piece of apparent stupidity may be accounted for by the circumstance that this reptile has no enemy whatever on shore, whereas at sea it must often fall prey to numerous sharks. Hence, probably, urged by a fixed and hereditary instinct that the shore is a place of safety, whatever the emergency may be, it there takes refuge. . . .

But it was his careful study of the finches of the various islands that was to have the most profound effect on his thinking. As with the tortoises, the finches differed significantly from island to island.

The different species still shared many common characteristics: short tails, no musical song, nests with roofs, color, and number of eggs. Their plumage varied, but only between black and gray-green, according to their sex and whether they lived among the greens of the moister high regions or amid the black lava.

The enormous variety of the finches' beaks attracted Darwin's notice particularly. The tree

The marine iguanas of the various islands have different colorations and markings. Those of Espanola are among the most colorful.

The yellow warbler (top), found on almost every island, locates most of its food by searching in the vegetation, such as this tangle on Floreana.
The color of the bills of the cactus finch (bottom) and other Darwin's finches indicate their readiness for breeding. Those with black bills are in a breeding condition, those with light bills are not.

© Rogers Assoc.

finches had beaks almost like those of small parrots, for pulling insects out of tree branches and eating fruit, flowers, leaves, and other soft plant parts. The warbler finch ate only insects and used its slim, pointed beak to pick these from the surface of leaves or lichens. The cactus ground finch fed on the young ovules of the prickly pear flower, using its long curved bill, but the thickness of the bill allowed it to eat seeds and a few insects as well.

The woodpecker finch had a strong, straight beak, but since it was not as sharply pointed as those of the woodpeckers, the birds used small twigs and cactus spines as tools to pry insects out of trees. The several ground finches had varying beak shapes that also related to their diet: mainly seeds of different sizes.

Darwin observed and noted all these birds and their habits, and these observations, coupled with the earlier fossil finds and other evidence, made him seriously question the prevailing creationist dogma. The fact that the finches differed not only from those of the mainland, but among themselves, suggested that they had been among the first species to arrive in the Galapagos and that they were for some time without competition for the food supply. This allowed them to adapt to the food and environment in each habitat quite freely. Had there been woodpeckers there, for example, already digging insects out of trees, this source of food would not have been open to them. The isolation of each habitat allowed new, specialized finches to evolve from a common ancestor.

Darwin began to develop the thesis that the world as we know it was not created in a single instant, nor in six days. It evolved and is con-

stantly evolving from primitive beginnings and common ancestors.

The Galapagos provided the perfect time capsule, enabling him to see this phenomenon in action and almost undisturbed. As an observant naturalist with an open mind he could not help drawing some conclusions from the puzzling questions they presented.

Why, for example, was the flora and fauna of the Galapagos so different from that of the Cape Verde Islands? They were similar in geology, climate, and physical appearance, but the living species of each were similar, not to each other, but to those of the nearest continent. If things had been created fullblown to suit their environments, why create two totally different sets of creatures for two very similar environments? And why make each so nearly like its own continental neighbor?

Another disturbing fact was that many of the recently introduced species thrived there better than the aboriginals. The native species were adapted to the situation as it existed, but did not deal especially well with changed conditions, especially new predators.

Then there was the question of the differences among the islands themselves. All these could be explained, Darwin was beginning to realize, by the theory that species can and do change. Galapagos flora and fauna must have originated from those of South America, and become modified in response to the conditions of each island.

Darwin had spent exactly five weeks among these strange islands, but he had seen and learned enough there to keep him at work for the rest of his life.

THE · EVOLUTION OF A · THEORY

As he classified and compared all the materials from his voyage, Darwin was "haunted," as he expressed it, by the certainty that all the various species had evolved from far fewer ancestral lines. In 1837, he began a series of notebooks on this subject exclusively. So sure was he that he was working on an idea of great significance that he outlined it in a letter to his wife, so that she could publish it in the event of his death.

The idea of evolution was not new; Darwin had read his grandfather's speculations and the woks of others who had considered evolutionary changes in life. But he was hardly caught up in the theory and was, in fact, so strong in his creationist convictions that he speaks of struggling hard with his conscience before believing his own evidence.

He knew also that his theory would raise a storm in Victorian, Bible-reading England, a furor he was reluctant to cause. Perhaps he also dreaded being accused of "darwinising," a term Coleridge had invented to describe Darwin's grandfather, Erasmus, when he had put forth similar theories. Charles, at least, wanted to have enough evidence to support his proposals to avoid this epithet for someone who theorized wildly.

It was twenty-five years after his voyage on the *Beagle* that Darwin shared his theory with the world at large. During this time he lived a quiet life close to home—he never again left England—and to his experiments and research. Much of this involved orchids, and through these and other species he amassed an overwhelming body of evidence in support of his theories.

When at last, in 1859, Darwin published *The Origin of Species*, the battle he expected began. Almost immediately everyone chose sides. The church had established the date of creation as the year 4004 B.C., and the Bible clearly stated that it took a week. It was heresy enough to suggest that the story of Adam and Eve was a myth, or at the least allegorical, but to suggest that man might share ancestry with animals was too much for most people.

Scientists and churchmen argued long and heatedly, and finally in a move that seems more in tune with medieval times than a supposed age of enlightenment, both sides assembled as though at a jousting match, with their best spokesmen carrying their standards, at a meeting of the British Association at Oxford in 1860. Leading the clergy was the glib but eloquent bishop of Oxford, Samuel Wilberforce (known to many as "Soapy Sam"), who had announced publicly that he intended to "smash Darwin."

Darwin was ill and could not attend, but his mentor, Professor Henslow, backed up by other eminent scientists, stood in for him. The battle

The ground finches, of which there are four species, are nearly identical in color, but differ in sizes and shapes of their beaks.

raged, with the bishop's eloquence so rich in contemptuous sarcasm that the scientists felt no qualms in telling him bluntly that he did not know what he was talking about.

From somewhere in the audience, waving his Bible, was Captain Fitzroy, shouting his own denunciation of Darwin, but in the hubbub, few heard him.

When it all subsided, no conclusions had been reached, but Darwin's reputation and following continued to grow. He was later given an honorary degree by Cambridge and applauded by the Royal Society. His theories were accepted and built upon, and eventually he became known as the father of modern biology. But the church was strong enough, even in defeat, to see that he was never knighted or given any official honor by his government.

Bright orange Sally Lightfoot crabs (above) scuttle about the wet rocks of the intertidal regions on several islands.
The varieties of California sea lion (right) found in the Galapagos are smaller and lighter than those found on the Pacific coast of the mainland.

Whatever the reasons that took the first visitors and colonists to the Galapagos, it is the wildlife and geological setting that attract the modern traveler and naturalist to those barren shores. Appropriately, too, for it was the wildlife and its peculiar adaptation to this insular setting that set Darwin to thinking, and it was Darwin who put the Galapagos indelibly on the map.

As a habitat for an unusual assortment of creatures and as a stopping place for seabirds, the Galapagos are unlike any other place in the world. There are few indigenous mammals, most of them aquatic. There are relatively few insects, no amphibians, spectacular reptiles, and an abundance of birds. The surrounding seas teem with a wide variety of life, from rare corals to immense whales.

Although it is easy to describe the islands, both in physical appearance and wildlife, as pre-historic, it is important to remember that the Galapagos are not a time capsule left untouched since prehistoric times, but a new and still-changing environment—newer by far than the nearby mainland. Even the islands' geography is in the process of change: in 1954 the west shore of Isabela (Albermarle) suddenly rose fifteen feet (4.5 m) and in 1968 the floor of the Fernandina (Narborough) crater dropped by a thousand feet. Volcanoes are active on some islands, long passive and weathered on others. Although the islands are all geographi-cally similar, their elevations, ages, climates, and sea currents differ enough to give them a variety of vegetation zones.

Swimming with the sea lions (left) is one of the highlights of a trip to the Galapagos, where the playful creatures are a common sight along the shore.

The shore area, known as the littoral zone, is only a few hundred yards wide, on the shore or the edges of saltwater lagoons. The latter are often composed of mangrove swamps. The area between the shore and the higher elevations of the volcanoes is the arid zone. This makes up most of the land of the archipelago, full of thornbush, prickly pear, and the palo santo tree, all plants able to withstand drought. The most common of these is the palo santo, which loses its leaves during the dry season.

In the humid higher zones, where the heavy fog gathers during the garua (cool) and drizzly rain season, there are mosses, vines, and taller trees, with the *scalesia*, or sunflower trees, the most prevalent. A sub-zone of this is found on Santa Cruz and San Cristobal, where there is a cover of low, dense shrubs and ferns. The higher areas, 1500 feet (450 m) and above, are relatively barren, sedge-covered expanses with no trees.

The origin of the marine iguana (above) is unknown, as is whether it was once a land species that turned to the sea or is the last remnant of a sea species.

Once the giant tortoise hatchlings survive the terrible odds of being eaten by predatory birds, they may live for a century.

© Fritz Pölking GDT

TORTOISES
· AND ·
TURTLES

The giant tortoise is the trademark of the islands. *Galapagos* is the Spanish word for turtle, and every early account contains the visitors' marvels at these giant reptiles. Found only in the Galapagos and on certain islands in the Indian Ocean, the giant tortoises are remnant species whose ancestors once plodded the mainlands of five continents and countless islands.

Eleven subspecies of the tortoise still exist on the islands, the largest of which can weigh over 600 pounds (270 kg). The shape of the shell varies according to the vegetation of their habitat. Those with shells raised at the front and back live on islands with sparse vegetation where, many scientists think, the increased "collar space" allows the neck to reach farther in search of food.

Dome shaped shells are less likely to catch on limbs and branches and are found on tortoises inhabiting the lusher areas, where food is also more plentiful and a long reach isn't as essential. An Earthwatch team recently studied these tortoises, following them on their foraging rounds—their study suggests that although foodreaching may once have been the cause of the different shell shapes, it no longer has any relationship to the diet or eating habits of the tortoise.

For centuries, man was a serious predator of the giant tortoises, capturing them to store live in the holds of ships, where they survived as food for long periods. Early colonists killed them for food and simply moved to another island whenever the tortoise population was exhausted. Since the tortoises have become protected, their predators are now those animals introduced by man, such as rats, which eat eggs and young tortoises, and compete for food plants. Introduced pigs root up the tortoises' nests and donkeys trample the nests and break the eggs. Dogs and cats also eat the young tortoises.

The female tortoise nests during the rainy season, digging a hole, where she lays two to sixteen eggs, covers them, and leaves them. The eggs require from four to six months to incubate.

It takes the hatchlings from a few days to weeks to dig their way out of the nest, at which time they are prey to both hawks and owls as they search for scarce plant food. But the tortoise that makes it past this difficult stage may live for over a century.

Saving the tortoise populations is a major concern of the Ecuadorian Galapagos National Park Service and the Charles Darwin Research Station. There are captive breeding programs

The marine tortoise makes this trail (above) as it goes ashore to lay eggs in holes on the beach, but newly hatched tortoises must find their way past predators, including crabs and birds as well as feral animals.
On the southwest side of Santa Cruz, there is a tortoise reserve where visitors, with a guide, may go on day trips or camp (opposite page).

for the rarest species, in which surviving males and females can be brought together, eggs can be incubated, and young reared until the tortoises are big enough to be released in the wild. Over two hundred and fifty tortoises have been repatriated to Española Island through this program, a population that, only twenty years ago, was almost extinct.

Efforts to protect them from introduced species are twofold: eradication programs are under way for the predators, and tortoise eggs and young are collected from the wild for rearing at the breeding center. Over 1000 three-to five-year-old tortoises have been returned to the wild on various islands. On the islands of Española and Pinzon, the oldest groups of returned young are now reaching nineteen to twenty-four years of age, are mature, and have begun to mate and produce nests and young. The conservation program is coming full circle.

The tortoise is well-suited to these islands, since it can survive for as long as a year on the water produced by fat stored in its fatty tissue. They are herbivores, eating only fruits and cactus pads.

The turtle has developed an interesting relationship (symbiosis) with the finches and mockingbirds, which remove parasites from the tortoises' skin. The tortoises combat ticks and mosquitoes by wallowing in mud holes and water, which are also thought to regulate body temperature.

The mating behavior can be very amusing to the observer, although presumably not to the tortoises involved. Because of the tortoises' difficult shape, the male occasionally falls off and lands upside down, from which position it has difficulty regaining its feet.

The naturalist M. H. Jackson, who has observed this behavior frequently, describes in his *Galapagos: a Natural History Guide*, how "Copulation, which may last for hours and is a noisy, creaky affair, has its own hazards.... Frustrated males may attempt to mate with other males and even with boulders!"

Observers are prompted to recall Ogden Nash's lines:

> The turtle lives twixt plated decks
> Which practically conceal its sex;
> I think it clever of the turtle
> In such a fix, to be so fertile.

The Pacific green turtle is a marine species, seldom seen except during mating season, when they gather in the lagoons. Jackson again describes the scene in inimitable prose: "The constant train of suitors must be exhausting for the females, and it is common to see them floating with one flipper hooked around a mangrove root or hauling themselves just out of the water to rest."

They lay their eggs in holes they dig on the beach, as many as seventy at a time. The hatchlings are prey to crabs, hawks, herons, and other birds, and also to introduced animals. Although they are usually hatched at night and make their way to the water, they are no safer there, with sharks, fish, and seabirds all preying on them.

IGUANAS

Darwin described the land iguana in less than flattering terms: "Like their brothers of the sea-kind, they are ugly animals, of a yellowish orange beneath, and of a brownish red colour above: from their low facial angle they have a singularly stupid appearance."

Residents of the drier zones, iguanas are as long as three feet (.9 m) and can weigh twenty-five pounds (11 kg). This species is found only in the Galapagos. They absorb the morning and afternoon sun while lying spread out on the ground or lava rocks, retire to the shade from the midday sun, and sleep in burrows to conserve heat at night.

The pads, flowers, and fruit of the prickly pear cactus are favorite foods, and provide moisture in the dry season. Sometimes they eat these sharp spines and all, but often roll or scrape them on the ground first to remove the spines. They live where there is normally little or no natural water, but will drink from pools that form occasionally during the rainy season.

Unlike the tortoise, the iguana is territorial, and the male of the species is notably aggressive. Females guard their nests, not only to protect the eggs, but to prevent other females from nesting in the same spot. The small baby iguanas are prey to birds, but once past infancy can live sixty years.

Iguanas were once so plentiful that Darwin had trouble finding a place without burrows that was large enough to pitch his tent on Santiago (James) Island. Today, entire populations of iguanas have been decimated by introduced animals. Pigs eat the eggs, cats eat the young, dogs eat both young and adults, and goats leave the land barren of food for them. When wild dogs (really feral dogs, brought there long ago and gone wild) wiped out all but about sixty of an iguana population that once numbered six hundred on Santa Cruz, the Darwin Station and Park Service rescued the survivors, took them to the breeding facility, and reared the young. After removing all the dogs, the Park Service returned the iguana population to the wild to continue its recovery.

The land iguana spends much of its time sunning on the lava rocks (opposite page), a boon to photographers, who are able to approach closely and catch the lizard in full sunlight. The land iguana subsists mainly on the fleshy thick leaves of the Opuntia *cactus (above) and is able to scrape off the sharp spines before biting into one.*

The openings in the nostrils of the marine iguana enable it to expel the salt from seawater in spurts of strong saline solution (right).

The marine iguana has a blunter nose than the land species. This feature, along with its serrated teeth, enables it to feed on algae and seaweed (above).

The marine iguana of the Galapagos is the world's only known seagoing lizard. They are about the same size as the land iguana and just as oblivious to man. Thought to have evolved from a common ancestor with the land iguanas, this species eats marine algae. Its tail is flattened sidewise to adapt it to swimming. The snout is shorter than that of the land iguana and blunt, the teeth are serrated, and the claws sharp and curved. Each of these adaptations enables it to cling to rocks and feed efficiently on seaweed. Since they drink seawater, they have two glands that rid them of the salt by producing a strong saline solution that they expel in spurts from openings in the nostrils.

They live in highly concentrated colonies in areas along the shore, where there may be more than 4,000 of them per mile. They vary in color according to their native island, some dark gray to black, the others bright reds and greens, but they are otherwise very similar and are considered one species.

Although not all the wildlife in the Galapagos can live together in a "Peaceable Kingdom" relationship, the marine iguanas and Sally Lightfoot crabs share the seawashed rocks without incident.

Both sea lions and iguanas spend considerable time sunning on the lava rocks along the shore, and neither seems to mind the presence of the other.

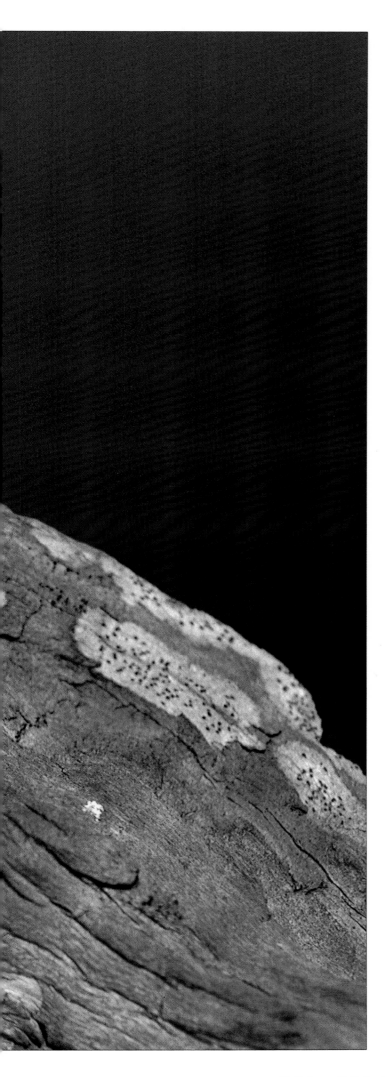

LAVA · LIZARDS

Found all over the arid regions, these lizards may grow up to a foot (30 cm) in length and are of various colors and patterns. They eat grasshoppers, spiders, beetles, moths, and other insects. They are well suited for hunting these creatures, because they have excellent eyesight. Snakes, hawks, and herons are their predators and a lizard escaping from one will often cast off its tail to confuse the predator, growing a new, but shorter, tail in its place.

Eggs are laid in dug nests. The baby lizards are so well camouflaged that they escape the notice of many of their predators.

Geckos, small nocturnal lizards with bulging eyes, and a few nonpoisonous varieties of snakes complete the reptile roster.

Only one species of lava lizard is found on any single island, but they are generally thought to be descended from a common ancestor (below).

It is easy to see the relationship between the lava lizard and the iguana by their similar shapes. They are commonly seen perched on rocks waiting for insects (left).

SEA · LIONS · AND · FUR · SEALS

One of the many surprises for unprepared visitors to the Galapagos is the presence of so many creatures usually associated with colder climates. The Humboldt current brings cold water to the Galapagos and with it, such species as sea lions and penguins.

The playful sea lions are particular favorites with visitors, since they swim with almost total unconcern for human bathers among them. They have left smoothly polished trails on the rocks from which they have slid so often into the water, and they are great fun to watch as they cavort in the sea with their pups.

Unlike the penguin and fur seal, whose ancestors moved north with the Humboldt current, the sea lions are a smaller species of those found in California, and are thought to have come to the Galapagos during a glacial age when colder currents reached the islands from the north as well as the south. Even though they are smaller than the California sea lions, a male here may weigh 500 pounds (225 kg).

Each male has a territorial colony of up to thirty cows and their young. The bull's territory is a stretch of coastline, which he guards zealously by swimming up and down it constantly, fighting off other males who try to invade. But this vigilance takes its toll, leaving the male no time to feed. When a dominant male becomes too weak (usually after four to eight weeks) to fight off a roving bachelor, he loses his territory and joins a bachelor colony until he is strong enough to take over another colony of females.

Pups are born singly and nursed for one to three years, but females can conceive each year and rear and feed pups of different ages. While mothers are fishing, a number of young pups will congregate, with a single female nanny watching over them. The male sea lion patrolling his shore always warns pups of approaching sharks and sometimes chases the sharks back out to sea.

Sea lions group in rookeries with cows, bulls, and pups living together. Groups of "bachelor" sea lions live in all-male colonies (opposite page). Above: Each male sea lion, right, may have a territorial colony of as many as 30 cows, with their pups.

Unlike the California sea lion, the fur seal does not welcome human company and lives on cliffs where it is difficult to approach.

Although sharks are the sea lion's only predators, they have a viral disease (a pox) which occasionally causes high mortality throughout the population. However, resistant individuals survive and breed, bringing the population up to former levels within a few years.

Fur seals live in rocky sea cliffs, where there is more shade and cooler water, since they are descended from creatures of the cold Antarctic and southern shores of South America. Smaller than the sea lion, with a broader head and pointed nose, the fur seal's front flippers are actually larger, making it a better climber than the sea lion.

The coat of the fur seal is denser, thicker, and more insulated, well designed for Antarctic waters, but uncomfortable for the Galapagos in the heat of the day. The thick coat proved an even greater threat to the fur seals' survival, however, because it was very highly prized by furriers. Tens of thousands of fur seals were killed by hunters in the 1800s, severely reducing the population.

They are now protected and their population is increasing steadily. Even so, they are difficult for the visitor to see because of their cliff habitat. James Bay on Santiago is the best place for viewing these seals. Unlike the sea lions, the fur seals will not let people come very close, and slide into the water at the first sign of human approach.

With hunting prohibited, sharks are the fur seals' only predator. To make themselves less visible, the seals fish at night, and are most active on those evenings with little moonlight.

Their colonial, territorial, and breeding habits are much like those of the sea lion, except that the male guards his territory from the land, not the sea. Although the mother fur seal can bear a cub each year, a second pup will not survive if a yearling is still nursing.

Baby fur seals are not left in nurseries as sea lion pups are, and are frequently left alone by their mothers for as long as two days while the mothers are out fishing for food. On their return, the mothers call and the pups respond, each recognizing the other's voice. They then make their way to each other, the mother from the sea and the the pup over the rough surface of the lava on shore.

WHALES
· AND ·
DOLPHINS

It is always a surprise to learn that the diet of a very large animal is something quite small. The notion of a 30-ton (27-t) humpback whale subsisting on microscopic animals and plants is a difficult one to accept. The baleen whales, which include the humpback and fin, Sei, Brydés, and similar species of Galapagos waters, have a bone plate instead of teeth, through which they push the water and filter out plankton as it passes through. The toothed whales, including the sperm, killer, and pilot varieties, are also seen fairly often in Galapagos waters; these whales eat fish, squid, and other larger animals.

Once the richest whaling grounds in the world and a favorite spot of both British and American whaling ships, the area around the Galapagos is fortunately less suited to modern mechanized whale-hunting methods. For the present, the whale population there is not threatened by whaling.

Bottle-nosed and common dolphins are a frequent sight, and the former swim so close to the large tour boats that the passengers can hear their high-pitched dolphin songs. On moonless nights, the dolphins glow spectacularly as they swim along before the bow, in the phosphorescence caused by microscopic plankton.

Bottle-nosed dolphins are a frequent sight at sea among the Galapagos and swim quite close to tour boats.

Galapagos hawks
(above), the most
fearless of all the
birds of prey, will fly
quite close to
humans. Darwin
reported that, "I have
been shadowed by
young hawks for over
two miles."
The masked booby
(right) is the largest
of the boobies, with a
wingspread of over
four feet (1.2 m).

C H A P T E R · F O U R

T H E · B I R D S

SEA BIRDS

Thought to be the first form of life to arrive on the Galapagos, the seabirds also may have been responsible for bringing much of the flora to the islands in the form of seeds clinging to their feathers. Since most of these seabirds lay their eggs on the ground and require no plant materials for nests, the Galapagos in their open ocean would have been a welcome nesting place for these birds, which live entirely off the fruits of the sea. No predators were there to disturb their eggs or young, making the islands the perfect land base for their foraging.

There are well over half a million—perhaps as many as three-quarters of a million—seabirds in the Galapagos, including the world's largest concentration of several of the various species of boobies. To the visitor, the most surprising thing about these and other birds is their almost total lack of fear of humans. It is possible to wander among their nests, approaching close enough to photograph one of them without a telephoto lens.

THE · THREE · BOOBIES

The boobies include the blue-footed, masked, and red-footed, which often nest in adjacent colonies. They incubate their eggs not by sitting on them, but by standing on them with their large webbed feet. Colonies are densely populated with several hundred birds.

Even more spectacular than the sight of hundreds of birds with blue or red feet standing around on eggs is the sight of a single booby diving for fish. It appears to stop momentarily in flight to tuck its wings slightly and dive straight into the water, its long, thin beak pointed down. This long, fast dive enables the booby to go quite deep, and as it rises out again it scoops up a fish and swallows it.

The female (below) is distinguished from the male by the pupil of her eye, which appears larger due to deeper pigmentation.

The booby's long tail gives it extraordinary flexibility underwater, where it is able to change the path of its dive instantly. Because of this attribute, boobies are able to dive from great heights into very shallow water without injury.

Although the blue-footed booby builds no nest, the mating pair does carry out a curious nest-building ritual, suggesting that their ancestors may once have had nests. The male bird finds a bit of nest-building material—a feather or small twig—and brings it back in his beak for the female to see. He places it ceremoniously on the ground where the eggs will eventually be laid, and they move it a little this way and a little that way as if preparing a nest. No other material is brought, just these single simple tokens.

Perhaps this ritual is an indication of their intent to remain together until the young are independent, since both incubation and rearing are shared jobs. Labor is divided according to the special characteristics of each parent.

The blue-footed booby, shown on the opposite page with a chick, will only feed and care for its young if the chick stays within a certain distance of the nesting site. Chicks who stray will be rejected by parents.

Smallest of the three boobies, the red-footed booby normally has brown plumage, but a small number have white plumage, which makes them more difficult to distinguish from the blue-footed type.

The smaller male has more flexibility in shallow water and does more of the fishing when the chicks are small and require frequent feeding. But the stronger, larger female can travel farther and takes over feeding duties when the chicks require larger food and can wait longer between feedings.

The red-footed booby does make a nest, a sort of platform of twigs gathered by the male and arranged by the female in a low tree or shrub. Only one egg is laid and a parent will guard it for as long as sixty hours while waiting for the return of the mate, which fishes far out to sea.

The masked booby lays two eggs, three days apart, on the ground, like the blue-footed booby. The first chick hatched is therefore stronger, and physically throws the younger one out of the nest, where it dies of starvation. This happens in years of plenty as well as shortage, whereas a nest of blue-foots fight over food only when it is very scarce. The second masked booby chick is an insurance policy, as it were, in case anything happens to the first chick in its first few days of life.

Masked booby colonies are usually found on the outer slopes or sea cliffs where air currents assist them in lifting their heavy bodies into flight (below).

Masked booby chicks (above) grow as large as their parents before they begin to sprout feathers, and will not become independent or even feed themselves for a long period of time.

The American oyster-catcher (below) is found on the rocky shores and beaches where it eats crabs and mollusks.

The first part of the elaborate mating ritual of the blue-footed booby is the male's advertising his interest by pointing his bill straight up and holding his wings in an out-stretched position (opposite page).

FRIGATE · BIRDS

Although it is hard to envision a more striking sight than a bird with blue feet diving from sixty feet (18 m) in the air straight into three feet (.9 m) of water, the frigate bird is even more astonishing if seen during its courtship season. For the male of this species has a brilliant red pouch in its throat, which it inflates to attract females. An entire colony of these birds displaying their red pouches and calling in undulating whoops is one of nature's finest spectacles.

The frigate birds both nest and perch in trees and shrubs. Both partners share in building a rough platform of twigs, where a single egg will be lain. Parents alternate week-long shifts during the incubation and for the first week or so until the chick can be left alone.

For the next five months this chick sits on its platform in the sun, waiting to be fed. Even after that it depends on its parents for over a year. As a result, a pair of frigate birds can raise only one chick every other year.

Expert flyers, the frigate birds have enormous wingspans in comparison to their weight. These and their forked tail give them almost perfect balance in the air. They are able to make perfectly timed swoops, catching prey just at the water's surface. Unlike the booby, they cannot dive underwater without risk of becoming waterlogged and drowning. They solve this problem easily by letting the boobies and other birds catch the food, and then pirating it away from them. The frigate often gives chase to a successful booby, harassing it into disgorging its catch, which the frigate can snatch from midair before it hits the water. They also eat turtle hatchlings and unprotected baby birds—even those of fellow frigate birds— as well as squid, small fish, and other prey they catch on the sea's surface.

The frigate bird is perhaps the most dramatic of the Galapagos bird life. Here a male inflates his brilliant red sac to attract females.
It is hard to believe that this gawky frigate bird chick (above) will someday be the showiest bird on the archipelago.

The male great frigate bird (below) is difficult to distinguish from the male magnificent frigate bird, except for the slightly purple sheen to the former's back plumage.

PENGUINS

One does not expect to see penguins astride the equator, but the Galapagos is home to a tiny penguin (only about a foot [30 cm] tall) whose closest relative lives on the southern coast of South America.

These penguins swim at high speeds underwater, using their wings as propellers and forming rudders with their feet. They eat small fish that they capture by fishing in groups.

Like the fur seals, penguins must find some way of keeping cool in the tropical heat despite their thick layers of fat and heavy insulation of feathers. They do this by holding their wings out to cool their less heavily feathered sides and by keeping their feet shaded by their bodies.

Visitors can get their best views of the Galapagos penguins (below) from the pangas—small boats that take passengers ashore.

Although they live in colonies, penguins (opposite page) always stand and move separately, with a small area of free space surrounding each one.

When all else fails, they dive into the water. Penguin breeding is heavily influenced by the weather, with much higher success rates in cooler years and fewer young in warm ones.

These penguins mate for life and lay one or two eggs in nests made of circles of little stones set on the lava. They look as though they had been lain in that way to keep the eggs from rolling off into the sea. One parent always stays with the eggs or young. Penguins live in colonies, but each pair of penguins has its own nesting area that it will defend. They also have an acute sense of their own air space, an area around them that is theirs alone. When moving about within their colonies they have a peculiar head wag that is thought to indicate that they are in transit and not invading a territory they happen to pass through en route.

Largest of the Galapagos birds, the pelican (right) is usually the first one seen by visitors, as they congregate around docks and ships, hoping for food scraps. But they are expert fishermen, and are seen frequently on the uninhabited islands as well.

Brown pelicans (above) build untidy nests of twigs in low shrubs or in mangrove forests, where they lay two or three eggs.

THE · BROWN · PELICAN

So unconcerned with the presence of humans that it will build its large nest of sticks within a few feet of a building, the brown pelican is a common sight in the harbors as well as among the mangroves and the rocky shores of the Galapagos Islands.

The largest of the Galapagos birds, it has a wingspan as great as seven feet. Its walking, diving, and swimming movements are awkward to the point of being ridiculous, but this great creature makes up for it in the grace and rhythm of its flight. Its long neck is folded over its back and its huge wings flap in two or three leisurely movements before it goes into a long glide. Pelicans often fly right above the surface of the water, and when flying in a group they look almost like a precision team, gliding and using their wings in unison.

Their large pouches can expand to hold two gallons of water scooped up while diving into the water. The pelican then drains the water out of its pouch, leaving only the catch of fish.

THE · WAVED · ALBATROSS

Endemic to Espanola Island, all but a few pairs of the entire world's population of waved albatross nest there—some 12,000 pairs, mated for life. Unlike many of the seabirds that fish in short forays from the islands, the albatross flies away for four months, following the Humboldt Current to the western coast of South America, then returning to breed for the remaining eight months. Not only does the albatross not build a nest, it doesn't have a nesting site. The albatross moves its egg from place to place, over 100 yards (90 m) from its original spot. While it is not understood why they do this, it is known that frequently moved eggs have a higher hatching rate. When chicks are left, they group into

From early April through December, the waved albatross nests on Espanola. To witness even a portion of the elaborate and lengthy courtship dance is an unforgettable experience for the visitor.

nurseries, each returning to its own parent in response to the parent's call.

The long, slender wings of the albatross are ideal for gliding—by choosing their altitude (and hence their wind speed), they can soar for hours. They do have a problem taking off from level land or calm sea without the wind to give them thrust, and have frequent landing accidents when coming in on the rock-strewn lava runways at the high speed they must maintain for control.

© Fritz Pölking GDT

The tail streamers of the red-billed tropic bird are often as long as the bird's body, a dramatic sight against the deep blue sky.

THE · RED-BILLED · TROPIC · BIRD

The red bill and long white streamerlike tails of the tropic bird make it a striking sight, especially when seen in its nesting colonies against the dark cliffs, or circling above the sea. These birds travel between their nesting grounds in the Galapagos and the coast of Central and South America.

Their tiny feet sit so far back on their bodies that standing or walking is impossible. In the rare instances when they must move about on their cliffs and ledges, they scoot along on their breasts, pushing with their little feet. Takeoffs are easy from the steep cliffs: they simply push off by leaning forward from the cliff's edge.

The shrill whistle of the tropic bird reminded early sailors of the boatswain's whistle, so they named it the bosunbird. The Latin name derives from Phaeton, son of Apollo, who hurtled into the sea from the sky, an association suggested by the bird's takeoff style.

THE
FLIGHTLESS · CORMORANT

It is difficult to describe the wildlife of the Galapagos without using superlatives, but the most difficult title to award would be that of the most unusual. To many bird enthusiasts, that title would go to the peculiar flightless cormorant. As its name suggests, its rudimentary wings are not capable of flying.

The trade-off is that without the large wings it can swim with tremendous agility. The cormorants' strong feet propel them along the sur-

The flightless cormorant builds a large nest of seaweed in colonies along low rocky shore areas (opposite page). The greatly reduced

wing structure of the flightless cormorant is easily seen in comparison to that of this cormorant in Everglades National Park (below).

face, then they make jackknife dives to the bottom for food. Even though they don't need to dry their wings as flying birds must, they have retained this habit from ancestral birds who once flew.

They build large nests of seaweed in colonies along the shore. Their elaborate courtship dance takes place in the water as they swim around each other, raising themselves partly out of the water, flapping wings and shaking.

The cormorants are an interesting study in evolution, since it is easy to compare them to cormorants of other environments where loss of flight would have made the birds vulnerable to predators. Darwin concluded after studying the birds here that, like the giant prehistoric *Dinornis robustus*, wings might be a distinct disadvantage to large birds on ocean islands, where the winds of a sudden storm might blow them out to sea.

OTHER · SEABIRDS

The dark-rumped petrel is the most endangered bird species in the Galapagos, and although there is still a good-sized population of petrels, introduced dogs, cats, rats, and pigs eat both young and adult birds as they nest in the highlands of several islands. The population has been declining over the last century and only a major conservation effort by the Darwin Station and Park Service is helping to begin to reverse that trend.

Storm petrels, often called Mother Carey's chickens, are plentiful and often seen hunting in the wake of boats.

Of the several gulls, the swallow-tailed is the most striking, with its red feet and eye ring against its white, gray, and black plumage. Most of the world's population of swallow-tailed gulls is located in the Galapagos. The lava gull is also found only in the Galapagos, but is the world's rarest, with only about 400 pairs existing.

The swallow-tailed gull has a wide variety of calls that vary from a screaming gurgle to an almost plaintive cooing.

Young swallow-tailed
gulls (left) take up to
five years to reach
maturity and breed-
ing age, with almost
the entire breeding
population living in
the Galapagos.
Found only in the
Galapagos, the lava
gull's gray plumage
(below) blends easily
into the surrounding
lava rocks.

The great blue heron is a shorebird that nests in the mangroves in pairs or small colonies.

The Galapagos mockingbird (right) has a variety of calls, but none of these mimics the call of other birds, unlike North American mockingbirds.

The Galapagos dove was a major food source for early sailors and settlers because these birds were so tame and easy to catch.

LAND · BIRDS

Although there are not many species of land birds to be found in the Galapagos, most are endemic (that is, unique to the Galapagos). While this is not surprising, since tropical land birds tend not to be long-distance flyers (having no need to migrate long distances), it makes it especially difficult to understand their origins in the islands.

These land birds, in their isolation, continue to provide fascinating examples of evolution at work, just as they did for Darwin. The finches named for him are still the subject of extensive research.

The yellow-crowned night heron (below) eats insects, centipedes, scorpions, and even good-sized crabs.

The lava heron (left) is well-named, since its gray color blends almost perfectly with the lava.

The Galapagos dove is found on all islands. Darwin described these birds as landing on his hat and arms. Early visitors seemed to have slaughtered these gentle birds at a whim, and colonists relied on them for a regular food supply well into the 1960s. Despite this, the dove is still plentiful, especially where introduced cats are rare.

The mockingbirds of the Galapagos are predators, killing and eating young finches and lizards as well as eating any unattended eggs. They have a particularly interesting social structure, with a well-defined pecking order, and breeding groups that include a pair of parents and their previous broods to assist in rearing subsequent broods. These groups of related individuals establish and defend group territories—such behavior constitutes an extremely rare phenomenon in the natural world.

There are six heron species in the Galapagos, of which one is migrant. The largest is the great blue heron, and the only endemic one is the lava heron, its dark feathers almost invisible against the rocks.

Flamingos are frequently seen feeding on shrimp and tiny crabs in the lagoons. Their nests are unusual structures built of mud, but since the flamingo is easily alarmed, visitors are requested not to go near them, especially in breeding season.

The flamingos (above) of the lagoon on Floreana's Punta Cormorant are a brighter pink than those of any other place in the world, as a result of their diet of shrimp and tiny crabs.

The cactus finch has a probing bill well-equipped for edge crushing, and lives mainly on plant foods, such as the Opuntia *cactus.*

DARWIN'S · FINCHES

Probably the most studied and the best known of the Galapagos birds are its finches, which featured heavily in Darwin's *Origin of Species*. In 1947, David Lack made a detailed study of the finches, and based on Darwin's theory, explained exactly how the thirteen species of Darwin's finches evolved from a single ancestral species that had originally colonized one of the islands.

In the first stages, the population increased its numbers and made a few adaptive changes to island conditions. At this point the finches may have been the only land birds there, or one of a very few species. Some finches then moved to another island and began a second population. They, in turn, adapted to the environment there. At this point, the different populations began to look different, having developed colorings to help them blend in with different landscapes, and physical features that enabled them to make the most of the available food supply.

Even after the birds had moved between the islands to colonize, they continued to move, but now encountered different varieties. When these were not too similar they interbred, but natural selection weeded out their progeny,

favoring those that bred with their own kind. As a result, the groups remained separate and kept their varied feeding habits. On an island, this would have been an important feature, since it prevented them from competing for a limited food supply. Two or more species of common ancestry could then inhabit the same island, without competing for the same resources.

Each time this process was repeated, natural selection favored those birds with the most diverse and specialized feeding skills so that there would be a feeding niche for them. Or, more properly, the available feeding niche determined which features—usually beak length and shape—would survive and which would die out in each species.

Because each individual passed on a great percentage of its own peculiar traits to its desendants, the slightest improvement gave those descendants a tremendous advantage in surviving and reproducing in the environment. Adaptive traits were quick (comparatively) to develop and stayed distinct. The total isolation from the mainland birds made the Galapagos a perfect laboratory for evolution, with a highly controlled environment.

The finches we know today vary in size, color, and the shape of their beak. It is the latter that is the most surprising, given the relatively short time (in evolutionary terms) that they have had to develop since their common ancestor arrived.

Some bills are adapted for grasping, some for probing, and others for crushing. Some finches eat mostly plants, others mostly insects. The sharp-billed ground finches of Wenman Island feed on the blood of the boobies, which they draw by pecking at the skin while standing on the victim's back. On other islands, finches eat parasitic ticks from the skin of tortoises and iguanas, to the benefit of both.

The woodpecker and mangrove finches have developed a unique style of removing insect larvae deeply lodged in trees. They use a thin twig or thorn as a tool, holding it in their strong beak, to pry the morsel out of its hole.

The songs of the different finches vary, probably in response to different environments: a sound that carries well in the thick brush is different from one that can be heard across the open lava fields. The different songs reinforce their breeding habits by helping finches distinguish their own kind for mating.

Although the finches have been observed and studied ever since Darwin, little has been done to track their pre-Galapagos ancestry. David Steadman, formerly of the Smithsonian Institution, has tackled this study—a difficult one because the Galapagos finches have changed so much that they probably have little in common with their ancestors, if these still exist. Although quick to point out that proof is impossible without a fossil, and remains are unlikely to be discovered in the fast-changing volcanic surface, Steadman makes a very good case for the blue-black grassquit, a finch found throughout Central and South America.

Steadman writes:

> The grassquit is a bit smaller than most of Darwin's finches, though its relatively longer wings and tail make it a better flier, one capable of making the flight from the mainland to the Galapagos. Once in the archipelago, it would have developed the reduced wing and tail common among island birds, which often lose their ability for long-distance flying. Despite this small difference in size, the similarities in skeletons and plumage (shared by no other mainland finches), as well as some shared behavioral patterns, convinced me that the blue-black grassquit was the long-sought ancestor of Darwin's finches. Not all scientists have agreed with me, but concur that the blue-black grassquit offers a reasonable answer to a perplexing riddle.

Ground finches are distinguished only by their size and the shapes of their bills, which are well-adapted for crushing the seeds and plant foods that constitute their principal diet.

HOW · DID · THESE · SPECIES ARRIVE?

While it is easy to envision microscopic fern and lichen spores windborne, or seeds from the South American shore clinging to the feathers or en route through the digestive tracts of birds, it is much harder to imagine a giant tortoise or iguana arriving from the mainland 600 miles (960 km) away. Birds, yes, but land reptiles?

Yet scientists are convinced that all these living creatures arrived by sea, not by land bridge or even a string of islands that the reptiles might have "hopped" like a tourist on a Caribbean cruise ship. Even today there remains evidence in the rivers of the mainland to support this theory and explain how it happened.

During the torrential rains, rivers overflow and undercut their banks, dislodging huge single trees and entire clumps of vegetation, their bases a tangled mass of roots so intertwined that they not only hold together, but support soil and smaller plants. To these cling insects, an occasional hapless rodent or reptile, or even rain-soaked birds and mammals.

© Rogers Assoc.

Most of these clumps are scattered in their dizzying journey down the swollen rivers and the few that survive as far as the open sea, break up and sink there, leaving only the floating tree trunks. But occasionally there is a mass so entangled that it forms a substantial raft that is caught in the Humboldt Current almost the moment it reaches open sea. This is the same current that brought most of the early human visitors to the Galapagos.

The Humboldt Current sweeps past and through the Galapagos, and it still brings debris from the mainland with it, debris that lodges on the ragged island shore or washes up on its beaches. Dampier mentioned finding foreign plants: "On several parts of the shore there was driftwood of a larger size than any of the trees that grow on the island; also bamboos and wild sugarcanes, with a few small cocoa nuts at full growth though not larger than a pigeon's egg."

That rafts of vegetation can and do float great distances in the ocean currents is well documented elsewhere, and such living rafts are a fairly common sight in the sea off Guayaquil, the nearest mainland point to the Galapagos.

The chances are not great for one of these rafts to wash ashore with its passengers intact, but it is quite possible. Given the length of time involved, with an annual rainy season and a regular current, the probability of life eventually arriving becomes greater. It is still a very haphazard way to populate an archipelago, depending on chance to supply pairs of the same species, and ones that can adapt and find food in an alien world. But with enough time it could happen, and over millions of years, evidently it did. With each new arrival, the task of finding food, mate, and breeding ground became a little easier, the environment a little less barren.

The arrival of larger reptiles in this way is a little harder to grasp, but there are several possibilities. The first is that the first arrivals, especially the tortoises, were smaller, either a smaller ancestral species or young specimens. As we have seen, tortoises can go for months without food or water. It has been estimated that only five successful journeys in a million years could have resulted in the present reptile species inhabiting the islands.

The uneven distribution of life in the islands—the fact that it has no amphibians, only small,

Opposite page: It is difficult to imagine that living creatures, especially large ones, could survive being washed out to sea, drifting in the Humboldt Current for over six hundred miles and landing in the crushing surf on barren rock shores. Yet the sight of these large "floating islands" (this page) drifting out to sea from the river in Guayaquil makes the arrival of reptiles in the Galapagos a little more understandable.

Left: Even a single nest of reptile eggs, far more sturdy than those of amphibians, landing with the protection of the thickly tangled roots of a floating island could have hatched to become the ancestors of an entire species.

tenacious, indigenous land mammals, few insects, few snakes, and only a fraction of the vast variety of flora and fauna of the mainland would also be explained by rafting, since only certain species, such as the tough-skinned reptiles, could have survived the trip. Reptile eggs are more resistant to harsh environments than those of amphibians, and a single nest of these, arriving and hatching without predators, would have been enough to establish a colony.

Insects such as the carpenter bee and burrowing beetles could have arrived in floating logs, as could seeds and live plants such as mangrove, which can tolerate seawater. Birds are natural colonizers, and in the last two hundred years there are ample records of birds migrating permanently to South Pacific islands and the Galapagos—the cattle egret is an example. Non-resident birds turn up regularly in the Galapagos, some blown off course by the wind, others for unknown reasons. The prevailing winds from the continent would help in bringing both birds and flying insects.

The presence in the Galapagos of swimmers, such as the seals, sea lions, penguins, and sea turtles, is easy to account for, as are the abundant seabirds, which in turn brought a large percentage of the flora.

The arrival of birds, even those that normally do not travel great distances by sea, is easier to understand. In recent times, the cattle egret (above) migrated permanently to the Galapagos and established a colony.

The marine iguana
(above) is an out-
standing example of
a creature that has
found its own niche
in the Galapagos
ecosystem. Although
it shares its territory
with the sea lion
(right), they do not
compete for food
sources, nor even for
space to sun on the
rocks.

Every bit as interesting as the individual species are the ways in which they relate to each other and the land they live on. Predators and prey, plants and animals, rain and sun all play their part. Because the islands are not lushly forested and because they are so far from other land, food is scarce and replenishes itself slowly. Each species must find its niche in order to survive.

Different species work together toward their mutual survival. Birds eat bothersome parasites from reptiles, and every last scrap is waiting to be consumed, such as the noddy waiting for the pelican to drop a morsel of fish from its pouch-like beak. Every casualty, even the accidental ones, becomes another creature's dinner. Parents are engrossed with the business of feeding their young, while protecting them from other species that would prey upon them.

Insects eat plants, lava lizards eat insects, snakes eat lava lizards, and hawks eat snakes. But along with the food chain and its divisions, there are other facets to the ecosystems. Each species finds its own place in geography as well, with different birds nesting in different environments. Each fills a previously unclaimed space and then further adapts to it. A good example of this process is found in the habits of the marine iguana, which, having committed itself to the tidal and coastal area, is unable to live inland. In its narrow habitat is the seaweed it eats, and sunbaked lava where it can regain its body heat after forays into the cold water. There are no natural predators, and no other creature nesting or feeding in this region. In this unique place, the marine iguana has found its ecological niche.

Although each species has found a place and a food source, predation is a part of the food chain. To protect their young from birds of prey, masked boobies (left) take turns guarding hatchlings.

Flamingos (right) have found a plentiful food source in the tiny shrimp and other creatures found in the bottom mud of the salt lagoons.

While hawks eat the newly hatched tortoises, a full grown tortoise has no predators now that man no longer hunts them for food.

The carapace of a giant tortoise provides a favorite perch for the vermillion fly-catcher as it watches for insects on the ground below.

© Fritz Pölking GDT

TOMORROW'S · GALAPAGOS: A · FIGHT · FOR · SURVIVAL

Throughout any narrative about any facet of the Galapagos runs a theme so strong that it strikes with an impact almost equal to that made by the wondrous array of the wildlife itself. The theme is the omnipresent threat to the future of much that is wild and beautiful. Woven side by side with the many positive steps that have been made in the conservation of the islands is a long and terrible legacy of neglect and destruction.

It is not fair, however, to blame modern man alone for the wanton or careless decimation of wild environments. Although the Galapagos story begins in the sixteenth century after their discovery by historical man, aborginal groups in many other parts of the world have overutilized their resources and caused environmental damage prior to modern times. Long before the arrival of Europeans, island populations of Melanesia and Micronesia had eradicated a number of bird species.

The notion of conserving and protecting wild species is fairly modern, and it is not fair to condemn those early whalers and colonists from the mainland who killed the tortoises and the

doves and introduced domestic animals as predators to the rest. Conservation is a phenomenon born of loss: we only seek to protect that which is already depleted and in danger. In that sense, the Galapagos may be an exception, since efforts are being made to protect the environment while still mostly intact and before more than a few of its species are endangered.

Nor is it fair to assume that scientists have always been the protectors of wildlife; the opposite has occasionally been true. An expedition from the New York Zoological Society took 180 giant tortoises in 1928. It was common at that time for an expedition from a learned institution to declare that the few examples of a species they saw in a locale were lone survivors of a dying race and gather as many as possible to take home for study. Then the next group of scientists from another institution would find more, declare the species extinct, and carry those off.

The California Academy of Sciences expedition in 1905–06 removed eighty-six tortoises from Duncan Island (at least sixty of them females) after four previous expeditions had declared them nearly extinct and removed all the "last survivors" they could find. On that expedition, they removed a total of 266 tortoises from the Galapagos, representing all fifteen of the races then existing. They collected an astonishing 8,691 bird specimens as well.

Before blaming the Nantucket whalers for wanton slaughter, we should ask ourselves if taking the last of a species or subspecies for display or study is any better than killing thousands of a species for food or fur. Fortunately, such attitudes and policies are no longer in effect and scientific societies, museums, and similar institutions no longer conduct such collecting expeditions.

The same tourists who click their tongues righteously at the stories of the whalers of a century ago buy souvenirs in Puerto Ayora carved from the rare and precious black coral. Local residents continue to take the coral in response to the market demand, just as Chinese peasants will continue to kill pandas as long as wealthy Japanese will offer $20,000 for a panda skin rug. Conservation begins with caring, and caring begins with education.

By far the greatest threat to Galapagos wildlife today results indirectly from humanity. Mammals introduced there—often by accident—have thrived, gone wild, and now either prey on the native creatures or strip the land of their food supply.

Some of the first of these introduced creatures were the rats from ships, which promptly killed the native herbivorous rats. These had been part of the ecological cycle and had been kept in balance. But the introduced rats, being both herbivorous and carnivorous, now threaten both reptiles and birds. For the past century the rats have killed every single giant tortoise hatchling on Pinzon, leaving an aging population of that race without young.

Goats brought by settlers reproduced quickly and continue to strip the land of vegetation needed for food by native animals and to protect the fragile soil cover. Goats reproduce at a phenomenal rate. From three goats introduced on Pinta Island, the population grew to 20,000 to 30,000 in just fifteen to twenty years. On several small islands the cactus stands have been destroyed and former highland forests have turned into grasslands.

On Santiago, pigs brought by colonists and since gone wild simply wait for turtle eggs to be lain and take them before they are even buried. The pigs' acute sense of smell draws them directly to any hatchlings they might have

Despite the ban on harvesting the rare black coral in the Galapagos waters, coral vendors continue to sell it on the streets of Puerto Ayora. They insist the jewelry they sell is made of coral from other sources, and it is difficult for authorities to prove otherwise. Yet the coral fields continue to dwindle.

missed. Survival rate for the turtles is less than three percent. Wild dogs attack iguanas, killing them by the hundreds. This threat, combined with the attacks of pigs on the iguana eggs and young, has caused the entire land iguana population of Santiago to be exterminated. Wild dogs run in packs and will attack people as well as wildlife.

Control of these animals seems to require search-and-destroy tactics—very difficult in a terrain that is almost impenetrable. Hunting by local residents on inhabited islands is encouraged, and the park wardens make regular concerted extermination forays, but on the larger islands this strategy is difficult to implement.

Goats have been eliminated from five of the smaller and medium-sized islands, but campaigns on the larger islands may require a major influx of both manpower and funds, and success is by no means assured. Pigs are even more difficult to control because they are intelligent, reproduce quickly, and are most active at night, dawn, and twilight, when it is the hardest to hunt them.

Wild dogs, too, are most active after sunset and before sunrise, eating iguanas that sleep on the lava rocks. Eradication of these dogs is difficult but possible: it has succeeded on Floreana and San Cristobal and has begun on southern Isabela (where it is very important to remove them before they spread to endanger the large wildlife population on the northern shores), and on the northwest side of Santa Cruz.

Black rats are almost impossible to control, except on the smallest uninhabited islands such as Bartolome. A concentrated trapping and poisoning program succeeded there in 1976, but such an operation is difficult in larger areas with other animal populations that might be injured in the process.

Like the introduced mammals, many plants and some introduced insects wreak havoc on native vegetation and plant and animal species due to competition, predation, and direct destruction. The smothering of native plant communities by introduced plants like raspberries, quinine trees, and gravas is an example.

The biggest threat of all, however, is the potential introduction to the islands of new foreign plants and animals. Those could pose previously unimagined threats and wipe out all the substantial gains of active conservation programs over the past twenty-five years. As more and more colonists migrate to the Galapagos, fueled by the tourism boom, the probability of new organisms reaching the islands, by both accidental and intentional human introduction, increases rapidly. Likewise, with greater traffic among the islands the chances of spreading introduced species once they are in Galapagos increases greatly.

As immigration to the islands spirals out of control at over twelve percent per year, increasing numbers of harmful plants and animals are being introduced to the islands.

It is known that at least fifty new species of plants, dozens of insects, a lizard, and one bird species were introduced to the islands by man in only the past seven or eight years. Some of these will convert into wild populations, causing the destruction of native wildlife and endangering the Galapagos ecosystem.

A related problem is the increasing pressure on local natural resources. Several species of trees (used for firewood, shipbuilding, and construction), sand from beaches (used in construction) and many marine species such as Sally Lightfoot crabs, octopuses, chitons, and other shellfish, are under grave threat in and around settled communities and even in protected park areas.

Likewise, the use of spearguns is spreading, threatening to ruin the fearlessness of the beautiful reef fishes. Fisheries are springing up,

Feral animals are a continuing threat to native populations. Wild dogs feed on iguanas asleep on the lava rocks (opposite page).
Even the Sally Light-foot crabs (this page) and other shellfish are in danger of destruction in those areas near settlements.

The pale wood of the palo santo stands out almost white against the dark lava rocks and soil of Floreana.

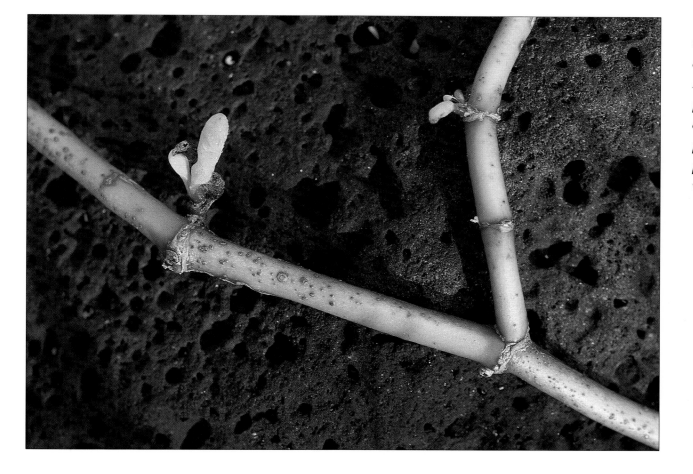

Tiny plants such as the Sesuvium that covers much of the lava rock have their place in the ecology of the islands and are protected from trampling by containing visitors to paths.

© Rogers Assoc.

The bare rocky shore areas are important as a resting place for sea lions who must rest and replenish their supply of oxygen after swimming in the sea.

including the netting of sharks for export of their fins, a practice which also kills sea lions and fur seals that get caught in the nets.

Because it has been well-controlled and managed, tourism to the islands overall has had little impact on the wildlife and natural resources of the National Park. However, now the tourism boom indirectly is producing severe problems of uncontrolled development and natural resource destruction in and around villages, and extending into the park and the surrounding islands.

In addition, pollution of the marine environment of the islands is rapidly becoming a problem as the number of tourist and supply vessels increases. Plastics, sludge from bilge cleaning, sharp-edged cans, fan belts, and other similar

items are the worst culprits. Plastic bags kill sea turtles that eat them by accident, mistaking them for jellyfish, and plastic disposable cigarette lighters choke albatross chicks to death (their parents pick them up having also mistaken them for jellyfish). Fan belts get caught around the necks of playful juvenile sea lions and strangle them as they grow older and larger. Cans severely cut fur seals and sea lions, while sludge and oil kill marine algae and invertebrates of all types. The shorelines of Galapagos, pristine only a decade ago, are beginning to accumulate the debris of modern "civilization."

Tourism, officially limited to 25,000 visitors per year, has actually grown from 20,000 only four years ago to 42,000 in 1988, and 55,000 to 60,000 in 1989. It is still largely well-controlled and managed by the existing system of trained guides, marked trails at visitor sites, and programmed itineraries for the large and medium-sized vessels. However, the system is beginning to show signs of breaking down with the advent of a second airport, more tourist services, and the installation of many new small hotels and day-tour operations. These are overburdening the few visitor sites nearest the ports on Santa Cruz and San Cristobal. The park service has opened all conceivably visitable sites in the National Park, but traffic flow of the myriad vessels is at the limit now. Any further increase will decrease the quality of the visitors' experience—that same sense of discovery that inspired Darwin. More vessels result in more crowded schedules, rushed visits on land, and larger numbers of vessels at every anchorage, as well as greater numbers of groups on shore at every site.

These trends bode ill for the Galapagos. Every other island or island group in the world where this has occurred has lost a large percentage of its wildlife and natural ecosystem. The Hawaiian Islands are good examples. However, in most of these cases tourism has continued as an economic mainstay due to abundant beaches and lush, tropical settings. Galapagos has neither, and the loss of its wildlife and natural beauty would be the death of the attraction that draws visitors there in the first place.

Concerted action by the Ecuadorian authorities with the support of both the international conservation community and the travel industry can reverse these trends so that the environment, wildlife, tourism, and local villages can all coexist in harmony. The existing, well-designed system for managing tourism must be improved greatly so that capacity stays abreast of tourism development. Policies must be carefully designed so that immigration, introduction of organisms, use of natural resources can be strictly regulated. The technology exists; willpower and collaboration of all institutions can get the job done.

Tourism to the islands, if properly controlled through management and educational programs, as was the case in the past in the Galapagos, can be a vital and positive force for conservation of the islands, as well as an economic benefit to Ecuador. Visitors contribute financially to the support of conservation and research in the islands through their donations and the park entrance fees they pay.

Everyone who comes to the Galapagos can learn something of the problems there, and return home to tell others. This process of education about wildlife and ecology is vital if we are to have a world population ready to step in and help during emergencies and willing to support programs for research and protection of endangered areas. There is no substitute for direct experience and to deny all but scientific researchers access to the area, as long as visitors can be managed and their numbers limited, would be a serious mistake.

Many who travel to the Galapagos out of curiosity return true believers, and their contributions of time and resources make possible the work of many of the organizatons which are saving and protecting these areas.

Once it has reached its adult size, the waved albatross spends its first four or five years before returning to the Galapagos to mate. The Tiquilia plant (following page) is a small herb with gray leaves that give it a ghostly skeletal appearance, especially during the dry season. It is often the only plant able to survive on the ash-covered volcanic slopes such as these on Bartolome, where it provides food for lava lizards.

WHAT · IS · BEING · DONE

As mentioned earlier, the Galapagos, for all their neglect in many regards, have been more fortunate than many other environments. As early as 1934, the Ecuadorian government enacted its first laws protecting some of the natural areas by declaring twelve of the islands a national park. Two years later two more islands were added. But, there were no enforcing officers and the laws were simply not very effective

site for the research station and reserves. In 1959, the International Charles Darwin Foundation for the Galapagos Isles (CDF) was established under the auspices of the Government of Ecuador, IUCN, and UNESCO. Its purpose was to advise the government on Galapagos conservation, promote research on the islands' conservation needs, and establish and operate a research center in the islands.

Based on the CDF's recommendations, in 1959, Ecuador passed a new, more comprehensive law establishing the national park. The entire archipelago was to be converted into a national park, except for those lands already owned by colonists, and the laws protecting the wildlife there would be enforced by resident administrators. In 1960, the CDF began operating the Charles Darwin Research Station, and practical authority for creating conservation practices and protected zones was granted to it. A plan for the control of feral (introduced species gone wild) ani-

Although most residents of busy, urban Quito have never been to the Galapagos, the government there has been rigorous in its efforts to protect the islands and preserve their fragile environment for future generations.

in protecting the islands from damage.

Ecuador was far ahead of other nations in at least recognizing the value of this unique area, especially remarkable since it was remote, both physically and economically, from the pressing realities in Quito. In the 1930s, they were already exploring the idea of a scientific research station and considering measures to control damage done by visitors. They asked for advice regarding these programs both in the US and Europe, but war intervened and international attention turned elsewhere.

In 1957 Ecuador requested advice from UNESCO and the International Union for Conservation of Nature and Natural Resources (IUCN), and a mission was sent to assess the islands' conservation status and recommend a

mals and another for designating a protected area on Santa Cruz for giant tortoises were first priorities. They also began the process of delineating boundaries for the national park, which would eventually cover ninety-seven percent of the land area.

The first officials of the new Galapagos National Park Service were sent to the islands, to begin a close cooperation with the research station, a relationship that survives to this day. Together, the two institutions have worked to preserve species, protect the environment, control feral animals, and set up a system for managing visitors. It was then that the determination was made to require all tour groups to be accompanied by a trained, licensed park guide, a rule that still exists.

Along with protecting the landscapes and ecosystems, the National Park Service was responsible for the control of introduced animals and plants, overseeing tourist activities, and developing educational programs for local residents and occasional visitors. The foresight and determination of the Ecuadorian government were especially notable because at that time there was no particular reward or benefit in sight. It would have been a noble act for a prosperous major nation, but it was one which required enormous sacrifice and commitment from a small developing nation such as Ecuador. Tourism was a far-off dream rather than a reality, or even a realistic goal, at this point.

No one could have foreseen the booming interest in environmental issues and conservation that the following decades were to bring. But when it happened and visiting the Galapagos Islands became a goal of nature enthusiasts, Ecuador was ready with a system to accommodate visitors and keep them from causing damage to the wildlife or its habitat.

The first target for education was the residents of the islands. The Darwin Research Station trained teachers and local officials, and natural history became part of the school curriculum. Guides were trained by the Park Service and Station to show visitors the islands and to impress upon them the vulnerability of the environment. Scholarships were offered for Ecuadorian university students to assist visiting scientists, who in turn trained them as researchers and conservationists and interested universities in their work.

By the 1980s there was a full resident staff at the station with an ornithologist, herpetologist, entomologist, botanist, and marine biologist, each working with a group of students, and all in conservation-oriented research.

The entire project has been a pilot without model elsewhere, and could only have occurred with the combined support of the Ecuadorian government and a broad array of international organizations.

After the initial stages, the cooperation of local residents has been impressive as well. The official policy has, wisely, been one of managing the islands as a whole ecosystem in which humans and wildlife are all part of the balance.

© Rogers Assoc.

The exploitation of native species was ended—no more baby turtles were sold as pets—and local residents were enlisted in programs to control introduced predators.

Farming and cattle raising are still the main sources of industry, and are centered on Isabela, Santa Cruz, and San Cristobal, where there are fertile moist zones. The way in which settlement agriculture and wildlife have been able to coexist to the mutual benefit of both people and animals is a further indication of the successes achieved through collaboration.

Today the Station and the Park Service face new challenges as they continue to search for solutions to the problems associated with introduced species, immigration to the islands, and tourism.

Luis Die of the M/V Bucanero is one of the naturalist-guides who must accompany all visitors in the Galapagos. Even small groups in private boats must have one of these guides, all of whom are trained at the Darwin Station.

SUPPORT
· FOR ·
GALAPAGOS · CONSERVATION

The annual budget for conservation and applied research in the Galapagos is a mere $900,000 U.S. (1989), of which approximately $600,000 is for research, training and education through the Charles Darwin Research Station and $300,000 for direct resource management by the Park Service. Since the two organizations work hand-in-hand the budget is, in effect, a single one. This is a miniscule amount when one considers that the CDRS has a staff of 60 and that they conduct a very large number of programs and activities. It would take eight to ten times that amount to do the same in North America or Europe.

By far the biggest single supporter over the past ten years has been the Ecuadorian government, which has supplied between thirty-five and fifty percent of the total budget most years. That has now dropped to twenty to twenty-five percent total due to the heavy loss (devaluation) of the national currency and inflation caused by the Latin American debt crisis.

The rest must come from international sources and most has to be raised year by year. With the help of the Nature Conservancy, approximately six percent of the total budget is now regularly contributed by the interest earnings from a modest endowment fund raised in the 1985-87 period. The remainder must be found by relying on a broad range of international organizations, the principal ones being the Frankfurt Zoological Society, the Smithsonian Institution, and the World Wide Fund for Nature/World Wildlife Fund—US (WWF).

However, the Darwin Foundation and the Park Service need a more stable and predictable source of financing if they are to be able to do necessary long-term planning. Presently, far too much of the budget remains unsure from year to year. With support from WWF and other organizations, the Foundation has embarked on major fund-raising campaigns in Europe, North America, and Ecuador, including funds for both direct operations and projects and the goal of a $10 million endowment fund by 1995.

Appendix II explains how individuals, groups, and organizations can help the Foundation to achieve those goals.

The Latin American debt crisis has had a serious impact on the amount of support the Ecuadorian government has been able to give conservation efforts to protect these landscapes and the life they support.

Although all visitors must leave the islands and return to their boats at sunset, there is still time for some dramatic photographs of the setting sun.

Charles Darwin observed in 1845, years after his own voyage to the Galapagos, that "Nothing can be more improving to a young naturalist than a journey in distant countries." To enjoy and appreciate the Galapagos, one need be neither young nor a naturalist, but one should have a keen interest in the natural world. Otherwise there is little point of hiking over sharp lava rocks to watch absurd birds with bright blue feet dance in the blazing equatorial sun.

Perhaps the Galapagos are best protected by their distance and by the effort it takes to get there. Visitors from North America can fly to Guayaquil or Quito via Equatoriana Airlines from Miami, New York, Chicago, or Los Angeles. A number of airlines (including Lufthansa,

Iberia, and Air France) fly Europe to Quito and/or Guayaquil. Flights to Baltra, the first airstrip in the Galapagos, are daily (one flight) except Sunday from Quito and Guayaquil (same flight). TAME Airlines flies that route. As of 1987, SAN Airlines has flights three times per week from Quito and Guayaquil to the new airstrip on San Cristobal Island, although connections from there are difficult to make. It is most important to have TAME and SAN reservations well in advance, since the planes are relatively small and there is only one flight a day. Cruise ships meet their passengers on Baltra or San Cristobal, depending on the different companies' itineraries, or, for passengers who wish to sail from the mainland, in Guayaquil.

Although cruising time from the mainland adds two days to the trip, there is nothing more exciting than arriving as did the early seafarers, hurried along by the Humboldt Current, first seeing the volcanic rocks rising out of the horizon in the middle of the vast empty Pacific. Travelers with a little extra time should not miss this opportunity to savor the full impact of arriving by sea. (And for many, two days at sea on a pleasant ship and in good company is far preferable to a two-hour wait in an airport.)

The choice of cruising vessels has become greater over the years. There are basically four types of visit:

- There are several large cruise ships which carry sixty to ninety passengers and which fall into the first class luxury category. This is a large enough group to be interesting and in which to find compatible fellow passengers, but small enough to have a casual, informal atmosphere.

- There are approximately ten ships which carry twenty to thirty-five passengers and vary from second class to very luxurious.

- There are some fifty to sixty yachts and smaller modified fishing boats (with basic conveniences), which are for the hardier traveler and carry groups of four to twelve passengers. These have bathrooms, simple dining facilities and other basics, but many lack showers. A few of these smaller boats, however, do have such facilities and are of the first or even luxury class.

- Finally, there are the day-tour boats, much smaller, open launches carrying five to ten passengers, which make only round trips by day from Santa Cruz or San Cristobal to relatively nearby visitor sites. These are rather uncomfortable and spend most of a typical six- to ten-hour day coming and going, with little time on shore at the visitor sites. Unlike the first three types of vessels, which are used as hotels by their passengers and follow itineraries of several days to weeks without returning to their home port, the day-tour boats have no bathrooms, cabins, or kitchens and cannot operate for overnight stays.

The porous nature of the rock on Espanola combines with the heavy surf to force geysers of water through the lava rocks at blowholes.

Pangas such as this one bring passengers ashore for morning and evening wildlife viewing. While some landings are made onto rocks or jetties, others involve jumping into waist-deep water.

All vessels, whether large cruise ships or smaller boats, must carry a registered, licensed guide trained by the Park Service and the Charles Darwin Research Station. Medium and larger ships carry one for every fifteen passengers. These guides are responsible for their group of visitors while they are on shore, for explaining the wildlife and the environment, and making sure that everyone stays on the trails and does not interfere with the wildlife.

Once ashore in small groups, the guides explain, point out, and answer questions about the many facets of each island's natural history. On Floreana, this might include its colorful, if grisly, human history as well. On other islands the guides will point out where to find the best blow-hole, the prime spot for snorkeling, the greatest concentrations of wildlife, and the best places for photography.

Typically the vessels make two stops a day, sailing between islands at night and during the hottest part of the midday. Island excursions usually occur in the early morning and late afternoon. All visitors must leave the islands and return to their boats at sunset.

Travel from ship to shore is by pangas, small motor boats that come in close enough for passengers to either jump or wade ashore. Some islands have "dry" landings, which involve jumping from a bobbing panga onto wet lava rocks (with the help of a crew member and a sure-footed guide.) Others are "wet" landings in which passengers slide off the side of the panga into water ankle to waist deep, then wade ashore to the beach.

Always be prepared to get wet to the waist in a wet landing. You may land at high or low tide and this governs how close to shore the pangas can get. Do not carry wallet, film, or notebook in pants pockets and use a plastic bag to protect camera equipment from splashing sea water and salty spray.

In preparing for a trip, it is wise to pack shoes appropriate for varying situations: a pair of sneakers for wet landings (some of the sandy beaches have sharp rocks before you reach dry sand) and a pair of thick-soled boots or shoes to change into once ashore. Spare sneakers, sunblock, and a hat are the most important things to bring to the Galapagos; fair-skinned people can burn in minutes under the equatorial sun. Bring light-weight shirts, shorts, bathing suits, jeans, sunglasses, and a waterproof jacket (if you are going to the highlands). From June to December, nights are cool and a light sweater is recommended in any event while at sea. Most ships prefer that passengers not wear shorts to the evening meal, but dressy clothes are not needed. Casual skirts and slacks are the rule. You can usually take your cue from the officers—when they change to "whites" in the evening, it is time to change out of shorts.

On shore, excursions are leisurely and not particularly strenuous. The National Park Service has made trails in those areas with the best wildlife concentrations and the guides take these at a leisurely pace with plenty of time to watch and photograph. Except for Bartolome, where the purpose of the trip is to see the view from the top, the terrain is gentle in slope. But the surface is often uneven, requiring a series of short, surefooted hops from one sharp piece of lava to the next. So thick soles and a little nimble footwork are helpful.

For this reason, as well as the necessity of climbing in and out of pangas, the trips are not suitable for those with physical disabilities that impair walking and normal climbing up or down stairs. Just getting on and off the ship each time requires climbing or descending a long steep series of steps, as does moving from deck to deck on board.

Tours are usually grouped into four or five day cruises, two of which may be combined to see nearly all the islands on the trip. The *M/V Bucanero*, for example, offers a typical ship itinerary including Santiago, Espanola, Floreana, Santa Cruz, South Plaza, and Daphne in one series and North Seymour, Isabela, Fernandina, Santiago, Bartolome, Rabida, and Santa Cruz in another. By staying aboard for both segments (eight days), one can visit twelve islands, repeating only Santa Cruz. But since Puerto Ayora has shops and cafes as well as the Darwin Station, it

© Rogers Assoc.

is a pleasant place to explore on the second landing. Many of the medium-sized vessels offer one- or two-week itineraries and the yachts and smaller boats offer any length desired from several days to several weeks.

Arranging a trip to the Galapagos involves land, sea, and air connections, all of which must be coordinated. The best way to make sure that you can get reservations on all of these various carriers, each of which has fairly limited capacity and high demand, is to plan well in advance and to book a complete tour that includes all those elements. That way you will be sure that you have the most convenient and reliable connections. The problem with making arrangements piecemeal is that if there is a hitch in one, you could miss subsequent connections.

There are many excellent and very reliable nature-oriented tourism companies and agencies offering tours of all types, lengths, and costs to Galapagos. Memberships in natural history societies, museums, and conservation organizations often include travel planning and these organizations frequently offer trips themselves. Many such trips are designed to highlight particular interests such as birdwatching.

See the Appendix for information on contacting agencies with Galapagos experience that can help you plan a trip.

The M/V Bucanero *(this page) is typical of the cruise ships that provide floating hotels for visitors to the islands. Landing parties are small, with groups of no more than 15 people in a place at one time.*

The landscapes of the islands, apparently sparse and barren, actually offer an infinite variety of sights for the amateur naturalist (following page).

Galapagos landscapes are, for the most part, low and barren, more rock than vegetation, but they have a strange wild beauty.

SANTIAGO (JAMES)

Known best for its dramatic lava flows, much of Santiago has had very little erosion to wear away the swirling surface patterns in the black rock. The major volcano is on the northwestern end of the island and smaller cones dot most of the rest of it.

James Bay has two anchor sites, one at Espumilla Beach, near a lagoon where flamingos can usually be found, and the other at Puerto Egas. Between the two lies a lava field, flowing to the sea in a fascinating series of textures and patterns.

Trails lead from Puerto Egas to a salt crater where there was once a mine, to a volcanic cone, and to the fur seal grotto. Visitors can swim in the grotto, where they will see a variety of beautiful fish as well as fur seals and sea lions underwater.

Galapagos doves and hawks, finches, and mockingbirds are the prevalent land birds. Both of these anchorages have wet landings.

At the east end of the island is Sullivan Bay, which offers a dry (but steep and often treacherous) landing on the spray-soaked lava cliffs. The lava here dates from early in this century and is the ropy variety known as pahoehoe. Lava cones dot the landscape and sea lions are common on the rocks and beach. The fine white sand here contrasts sharply with the black outcrops of rock. Blue-footed boobies and frigate birds nest throughout this area.

Espanola's flat surface is home to enormous colonies of birds, as well as sea lions that play in its surf (above).

ESPANOLA
(HOOD)

Although it is not as dramatic as neighboring volcanic cones, Española is rich in wildlife. It was formed when a block of lava rose up from beneath the sea, higher at one end, to form cliffs of over 300 feet (90 m) in height. The paths on Española are a series of rocks, often sharp, which make walking rough and tricky, but the terrain is generally quite level.

On the western end is Punta Suarez, where a path leads across a flat region alive with blue-footed and masked boobies. Sea lions swim at the landing area, where a white sand beach and crystal waters invite visitors to join the sea lions and cavort in the water. These playful animals will swim right alongside people, whom they seem to regard as other seagoing creatures to play with.

The cove is small, and the sandy beach is broken by sharp lava rocks, so visitors should wear sneakers when wading ashore, especially at high tide, when the water reaches up to the rocks. The path leads along the western shore, then cuts inland across the booby nesting

The sea cliffs at Punta Suarez take the full force of the waves, which force geysers (above) through holes in the porous rock. Beneath this constant spray, bright Sally Lightfoot crabs (right) scamper on the wet rocks.

grounds to the cliffs. Below is a fine example of a blowhole, where incoming waves create geysers through holes in the lava rocks.

On the cliffs near the blowhole there are usually a number of the island's own subspecies of the marine iguana, with colorful red and green blotches on their black backs. Bright red Sally Lightfoot crabs scuttle all over these rocks, and over the sleeping iguanas as well.

Farther on are the nesting grounds of the waved albatross, which nests only on this island. These birds stay at sea for as much as two years at a time before returning to Española for their elaborate mating rituals.

Finches, Galapagos hawks, and long-billed mockingbirds live amid the scrubby growth and thorny acacia trees. Swallow-tailed gulls and red-billed tropic birds nest on the steep cliffs.

Northeast is Gardner Bay, with one of the longest and finest white sand beaches of the archipelago. Visitors can swim with the sea lions. Gardner Island, hardly more than a big rock, rises out of the water just offshore. There is a wet landing at Gardner Bay, an excellent spot for observing occasional displays of group territoriality by the long-billed mockingbird.

DAPHNE

Visited primarily for its bird life, Daphne is a cone-shaped island formed of a single volcano whose crater contains another, smaller crater at its rim. The crater floor is literally covered with blue-footed boobies and the walls of the crater are full of holes where red-billed tropic birds and masked boobies perch. Frigate birds are found here as well although not in such abundance as the boobies and tropic birds.

Daphne Minor, not visitable due to its topography, is so eroded that its crater appears as a single cylinder rising almost straight from the sea. There is only a small depression at the summit, with a few palo santo shrubs.

The floor of the crater on Daphne is a major nesting ground (top right) for blue-footed boobies (bottom left) and its walls are covered with masked booby nests (bottom right).

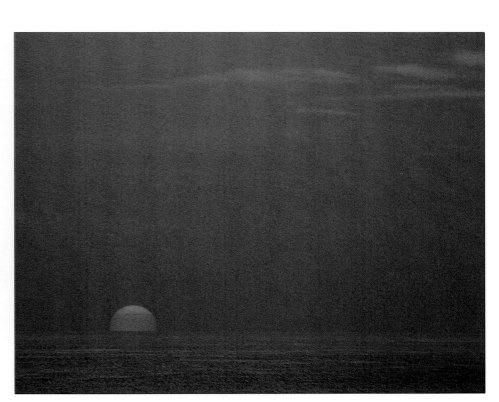

GENOVESA
(TOWER)

Among the northernmost of the islands, Tower lies a considerable distance away from most of the other islands, and, hence, is not often included in cruises. But its spectacular bird life makes it one of the most interesting islands. Tower is the top of a volcano cone, about two hundred feet (60 meters) in height, with a lake in the caldera.

Darwin Bay provides a wet landing on a coral beach. There are sea lions and small marine iguana, but it is the birds that most visitors come here to see. Swallow-tailed and lava gulls, red-billed tropic birds, shearwaters, noddies, both varieties of frigate bird, finches, doves, masked boobies, and the rarer red-footed booby are all abundant here.

The slopes of the volcano are not steep and are covered with Opuntia cactus and palo santo trees. Prince Phillip's Steps, a point encircling the eastern end of Darwin Bay, has a trail from the dry landing area where fur seals rest up the cliffs. At the top is a mile-long trail with superb views of red-footed and masked booby colonies, frigate birds, storm petrels, short-eared owls, finches, and other birds.

Although far from the other islands, Tower is a favorite destination for birders, who will see short-eared owls (far left), swallow-tailed gulls (near left), red-footed boobies, both frigate birds, and a wide range of others.

Floreana has a more interesting and varied landscape than many other islands, with long beaches, lagoons, slopes covered with palo santo trees, and green highlands (above).

FLOREANA (CHARLES)

The topography of Floreana is varied, with steep hills and small volcanic cones. It is one of the more luxuriant islands in terms of vegetation, most of which grows at its higher altitudes where there is considerable rain and rich volcanic soil. Much of the higher, wetter zones have been cultivated successfully ever since the settlers in the 1930s and 1940s carved farms out of its upper slopes.

Punta Cormorant has a long beach with a slightly green cast due to the mineral crystals in its sand. Behind this beach is a lagoon, sometimes almost dry, where the flamingos are the deepest shade of pink of any in the world.

A trail leads over a ridge through a light forest of palo santos, acacias, and Parkinsonia trees,

an area filled with the songs of the finches and various other birds that nest there. The trail ends at a white sand beach, a nesting place for sea turtles, which lay their eggs in the dunes behind the beach. Manta rays are common in the waters here.

Also on the north side of the island is the famous Post Office Bay, where mail is still left for passing ships to carry to its destination. There is a lava tunnel at Post Office Bay.

Las Cuevas Cove has another landing beach, surrounded by cliffs filled with caves and dramatic rock formations. Off Punta Cormorant is a submerged volcanic cone, heavily eroded by the sea, known as Devil's Crown. Tropic birds and noddy terns nest here, and the tropical fish make snorkeling outstanding. All these beaches offer wet landing sites, but sand paths make walking on the island easy.

More lushly covered in vegetation than most (above), Floreana is rich in sea life (below) and geologic interest as well. Caves are common in the sea cliffs as well as in the highlands where they were formed by lava tubes (right).

The Opuntia *cactus
(above) provides food
for land iguanas
(left), which eat both
its fruit and its thick,
fleshy leaves.
The great frigate bird
(below) has the wing
shape, precision, and
weight to make it one
of nature's finest
stunt pilots.*

SOUTH · PLAZA

A small but fascinating island, South Plaza is an uplifted block of submarine lava tilting gently from sea level at its north shore to perpendicular cliffs on its south.

The flat rocks are worn shiny in places by the constant sliding of sea lions across them. Huge *Opuntia* cactus trees grow here, and under them, land iguanas lie in the sun waiting for one of the large pads to fall off for their lunch. Although this variety does not ordinarily climb trees, as do the mainland ones, in times of severe food shortage some iguanas scale the trunks of the *Opuntia* and chew on the pads.

The rocks here are covered with a low mat of *Sesuvium*, which gives the landscape a red color. The trail leads up a gentle slope to the cliffs, which drop suddenly into the surf below. These high cliffs provide nesting sites for the red-billed tropic bird, swallow-tailed gulls, and storm petrels. Frigate birds soar in the wind currents without ever seeming to move their wings, rising and descending in the almost constant wind. Visitors should be careful not to walk too near the edge because of the sudden gusts that can throw them off-balance quickly, and the fragile cliff edge that can break loose.

Small yachts can easily harbor off South Plaza in the bay separating it from North Plaza (above).

125

Santa Fe is known for its forest of Opuntia cactus (opposite page), which grows to unusual heights.
Sea lions (far left) fill the water along the landing beach at Santa Fe, which is one of the best for both swimmers and snorklers. The island is also rich in birds, with nesting colonies of frigate and several other birds (near left).

SANTA · FE
(BARRINGTON)

Formed of lava crust which has been uplifted into an escarpment of steep cliffs, Santa Fe's geology is that of eroded lava. From the landing beach on the north shore, where an active sea lion colony lives, there is a short trail to a forest of giant *Opuntia* cactus trees.

Another longer trail leads upward to an area where land iguana are usually found. There are a few marine iguana on the shore rocks, but they may be harder to find. Along with the *Opuntia* there are palo santo trees. The terrain appears as a jumble of sharp, tumbled lava rocks, much eroded.

Bird life here is plentiful, with several ground finches, yellow warblers, brown noddies, pelicans, herons, mockingbirds, Galapagos doves and hawks, short-eared owls, and frigate birds. The surrounding sea offers parrotfish, mantas, white-tipped sharks, and sea turtles; the landing beach is considered one of the finest in the islands for swimming and snorkeling. Sea lions are especially sociable and are almost certain to join swimmers.

The only difficulty in going ashore on Bartolome is that over-friendly sea lions (left) often fill the jetty, leaving little room for visitors. Bartolome's Pinnacle Rock (above) is one of the island's most frequently photographed features.

The climb to the top of the crater on Bartolome is only moderately strenuous, with wooden steps built into the loose sand at the steeper final section (left). Early morning is the coolest time of day for this hike, when the morning light gives the scene even richer colors (above).

© Rogers Assoc.

BARTOLOME

Here, too, the sea lions meet passengers as they step from the pangas onto the black lava rocks at the eastern end of the island. From there it is a steady climb to the top of the crater for magnificent views out over the island and harbor and to the neighboring island of Santiago. From this height it is easy to see the sand beaches that border a low, narrow neck connecting the two parts of the island. A narrow mangrove swamp runs along its center. This lower area is reached from another landing and a trail connects the north and south beaches.

At low tide a submerged crater ring is visible below, near the docking area. Lava formations here are interesting, with several tubes clearly visible along the trail. "Bombs," rocks blown from craters, are scattered on the lower slopes.

Pinnacle Rock, with Sullivan Bay behind it, has become the "trademark" of the Galapagos, and is often featured in travel literature. The bay offers a fine anchorage, surrounded as it is by dramatic rock formations and islands. The sunrise here is especially spectacular, with rock profiles silhouetted against the orange sky. Very early morning is the best time to climb the crater, while the air is still cool, and the early sunlight gives the rocks a reddish color, offset by the deep blue of Sullivan Bay.

Penguins are often seen at the base of Pinnacle Rock, at the edge of Sullivan Bay.

Rabida is thickly covered in vegetation, which sets its landscape apart from that of many other islands in the archipelago.

RABIDA
(JERVIS)

Although only 1.5 miles (2.4 kilometers) in diameter, Rabida is quite high, with a 1200-foot (360 meter) dome. It has more varieties of lava rock than any other island and is covered with dense vegetation. The sand on the beach here is a rich red color. There is a flamingo lagoon on the northern side. Pelicans nest here, as well as blue-footed and masked boobies.

There are a number of different Darwin's finches on Rabida, and the brown pelican breeds here. Sea lions are common on the small beach and the waters are frequented by manta rays. The beach landing is necessarily a wet one. Since it is a small and somewhat difficult island to land upon, and it offers no wildlife varieties that cannot be seen more easily elsewhere, Rabida is not often visited. However, for those who do visit, there is excellent snorkeling in the waters around Rabida.

Rabida's beach is covered with rich red sand, a favorite place for sea lions to sprawl in the sun (above). It is also a major nesting ground for brown pelicans (below).

Fernandina has both dramatic geology and a wide variety of flora and fauna. Lava cactus (near right) accents the unusual lava shapes, and marine iguanas nest here in large numbers (far right). Tidal pools along the island shores are home to a wide variety of plant and sea life (opposite page).

Cormorants, penguins, terns, and hawks are common on Fernandina, along with the great blue heron, shown above with a sea lion.

FERNANDINA (NARBOROUGH)

A large volcano rises straight from the sea, and in company with neighboring Isabela, it comprises one of the most active volcanic regions in the world. An eruption in 1968 caused the floor of the caldera (crater) to collapse and sink more than 1000 feet (300 meters). The caldera there is over three miles (almost five kilometers) in diameter at the rim.

Lava takes on bizarre shapes and unusual colors at Fernandina and these forms are set off by the cactus and other vegetation which clings to its uneven surface. A trail from the landing area (dry landing) leads to the volcanic cliffs, rising straight off the beach at Punta Espinoza. Other trails lead through the edge of a mangrove swamp, to the lava fields, and past a number of lava tubes, natural underground pipes formed when the lava cooled on the surface but continued to flow underneath, where it was still hot.

A trail across a marine iguana nesting area leads to a point where there is a cormorant colony. There are penguins, pelicans, boobies, terns, herons, and Galapagos hawks. The largest population of marine iguanas in the Galapagos is here, and fur seals are common on the western side of the island.

SANTA · CRUZ (INDEFATIGABLE)

Nearly all visitors to the Galapagos go to Santa Cruz, either as a point of departure or to visit the Darwin Research Station. Puerto Ayora, in Academy Bay, is a thriving little town with a few pleasant hotels for those who are not staying on board a ship or who wish to extend their stay to visit the highlands. It has a few shops, cafes, bakeries, and a post office.

The Darwin Station has excellent illustrated displays on the history, geology, evolution, ecology and conservation problems and programs of the islands, as well as the breeding and raising facilities for the giant tortoises rescued from various islands. For visitors not planning a trip to the highlands, this is the only opportunity to see the creatures that have become the symbol of the islands. The Station is a short walk by road from the dock area.

In Puerto Ayora, visitors will see people selling jewelry made from black coral. If asked, the vendors will claim that this coral is not from the Galapagos, which is almost always untrue; and since black coral is rare everywhere, buying it simply encourages its depletion everywhere. There is a small shop at the entrance to the Park Service Headquarters and the Darwin Station, where posters, guidebooks, postcards, and shirts are sold, with the profits benefiting the conservation, education, and research pro-

There are two nearly identical, side-by-side craters on Santa Cruz called Los Gemelos (The Twins) (upper left). Travelers into this highland area will want to carry raingear, since the upper slopes are often enveloped in misty rain.

grams of the two institutions.

Santa Cruz has the most varied terrain of any island and hence the widest range of flora. The area around Puerto Ayora is covered by a thick forest of palo santo, *Opuntia*, matazarno, and manzanillo, with *Croton* bushes forming a dense undergrowth. Slightly higher, the *Scalesia* trees appear, mixed with matazarno and guayabillo. Beyond is a zone of thick brush, ferns, and bog that finally gives way to open grasslands near the summit.

On the southwest side of the island is a large tortoise reserve where visitors may camp or go on day trips. Arrangements can be made in Puerta Ayora to drive to the highlands with a guide. Along with the varied flora of the higher zones, visitors see bird life unique to this area, such as the woodpecker finch and the vermillion flycatcher, as well as most of the land birds native to the other islands.

Conway Bay, almost directly across the island from Academy Bay, provides a good landing place and features a population of land iguanas. Fur seals can be seen on Punta Carrion, near the channel between Santa Cruz and Baltra. Baltra itself has very little wildlife, having been used for most of the past fifty years as a military base and an airfield. There is a ferry connection between Baltra and Santa Cruz, which connects with a bus to Puerto Ayora. Passengers bound for the cruise ships are met at Baltra and board there.

Academy Bay (far left and near left) provides the busiest anchorage harbor for small boats, as well as the only center for tourist accommodations in the Galapagos.

San Cristobal's bird population is heaviest at Kidder Rock in Stephens Bay, where frigate birds (top left) nest along with blue-footed and masked boobies (right). The rarer red-footed boobies nest at the eastern end of the island as well.

SAN · CRISTOBAL (CHATHAM)

The town of Puerto Baquerizo Moreno on San Cristobal is the capital of the Galapagos Islands. Five miles away is Progreso, hardly more than a village. These towns lie on the higher southern side of the island, on the slopes of the San Joaquin crater.

This part of the island is densely covered with vegetation, and inland there are banana and orange plantations. A trail leads from Progreso (which is connected to Puerto Baquerizo Moreno by a rough road) up the crater to the freshwater lake of El Junco. The only year-round freshwater streams in the archipelago flow from this lake.

In the northern part of the island there is a surviving tortoise colony, but many of these animals have been destroyed elsewhere by the island's very active feral pig population. The lava cones on this part of the island are small and the rocky landscape is arid and barren. There are several beaches and landing sites (all wet) on this side, but most visitors make the dry landing from Wreck Bay into Puerto Baquerizo Moreno and climb from there to the crater and El Junco Lake.

Kidder Rock, also known as Leon Dormido, the sleeping lion, is a sheer rock rising nearly 500 feet (150 meters) from the ocean at the entrance to Stephens Bay on the north central coast. Frigate birds nest here, along with masked and blue-footed boobies. Red-footed and masked boobies, swallow-tailed gulls and frigate birds also nest on an islet near Point Pitt at the far eastern tip of the island.

ISABELA (ALBEMARLE)

More than half the total surface area of the Galapagos is taken up by Isabela, an island over seventy miles (112 kilometers) in length, comprised of six volcanoes whose lower edges meet to form lowlands between them. The northernmost, Wolf Volcano, is 5600 feet (1680 meters) high and is situated so the equator runs directly through its center. Five of Isabela's six volcanoes are active and over 2000 smaller cones dot the island. Alcedo Volcano, in the center of the island, has an active steam geyser and many fumeroles.

The Bolivar Channel is a very narrow strip of sea separating Isabela from Fernandina. In its cold waters, fed by the Humboldt Current, are Galapagos penguins and flightless cormorants, both unique to the Galapagos. Fur seals are also found on Isabela.

Tagus Cove is the favored landing site, a submerged ancient volcanic crater, now open on one side to the sea. It has provided one of the safest harbors in the archipelago since the days of the nineteenth-century whalers. Unfortunately, the beauty of the cove's steep crater walls was marred first by the carvings of the whalers and later by names painted there by sailors. There the visitor will find ash deposits, cones of lava, and a salt lake inside an almost perfectly round crater.

Puerto Villamil is the only anchorage on the south shore, a small fishing village on the edge of the lava fields of Sierra Negra volcano. A road leads from the docks up the slopes to the farming village of Santo Tomas. West of Villamil are fine beaches and mangrove forests, but there is no safe anchorage in the heavy surf.

The closest landing point for beginning the climb up the Alcedo volcano is at Shipton Cove, near Cowley Island. One of the largest populations of giant tortoises lives on this volcano. After a wet landing, there is an overnight climb to the crater rim. There are four campsites on the crater as well as one on the beach. On the other side of Alcedo is Urvina Bay, where the landscape is both dramatic and geologically fascinating. In 1954, in a single night, the shoreline rose fifteen feet (five meters) as a section of rocky crust was thrust upward. Flightless cormorants and marine iguanas live there, but the main scientific interest is in the newly formed cliffs. The landing there is a wet one.

The Galapagos hawk (above), found in breeding colonies on Isabela, has astonishingly good eyesight. Using a high limb or snag as an observation post, it can spot a small lava lizard at 100 yards (90 m) or more.

A P P E N D I X · I
V I S I T I N G · T H E · G A L A P A G O S

The major tourism operators in the Galapagos are as follows:

Canodros Company
Urdaneta 1418 y Avda. de los Ejercitos
Guyaquil, Ecuador
Telephone: (593) - (4) - 285711

This company operates the *Galapagos Explorer*, a 90-passenger vessel.

Galatours
1120 Barquerizo Moreno
Office 101
Guyaquil, Ecuador
Telephone: (593) - (4) - 321088

This company operates the *Bucanero*, a 90-passenger ship.

Metropolitan Touring
Casilla 2542
Quito, Equador
Telephone: (593) - (2) - 560550/560837

This company operates a large 90-passenger ship, the *Santa Cruz*; a luxury 35-passenger boat, the *Isabela II*; and several smaller yachts.

In the United States:

The Galapagos Center
156 Giralda Avenue
Coral Gables, FL 33134
(800) 331-9984 or (305) 448-8844

Overseas Adventure Travel
349 Broadway
Cambridge, MA 02139
(800) 221-0814 or (617) 876-0533

Inca Floats
1311 63rd Street
Emeryville, CA 94608
(415) 420-1550

In England:

Journey Latin America
16 Devonshire Road
Chiswick, London
W42HD
(01) 747-3108

In Canada:

Galapagos Holidays
745 Gerrard Street East
Toronto, Ontario
M4M 1Y5
(416) 469-8212

In Australia:

Contours
541 King Street
West Melbourne, Australia
3003
(03) 329-5211

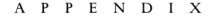

A P P E N D I X · I I

S U P P O R T · F O R · G A L A P A G O S · C O N S E R V A T I O N

The Charles Darwin Foundation for the Galapagos Isles (CDF); its research center, the Charles Darwin Research Station; and the Galapagos National Park Service are supported by national and international institutions, but remain dependent on the generosity of individual donors for the funds needed to finance their programs.

General Support and Specific Projects

In the United States, contributions should be accompanied by a note indicating they are "for conservation and science in the Galapagos Islands" and sent to:

> SMITHSONIAN INSTITUTION
> c/o Vice President for the Americas, CDF
> P.O. Box 37481-OBC
> Washington, DC 20013

This organization can receive tax deductible contributions from U.S. donors. No overhead is charged on contributions; all funds go to work for science, conservation, and education in the Islands.

Endowment Contributions

The Darwin Scientific Foundation, Inc., is a nonprofit organization devoted to building and managing an endowment fund from which the income is used for scientific research, education, and conservation of natural resources in the Galapagos. The annual income is used to support the most deserving activities and projects. Donations and inquiries should be addressed to:

> DARWIN SCIENTIFIC FOUNDATION, INC.
> c/o Smithsonian Institution
> Washington, DC 20560

This organization can receive tax-deductible contributions from U.S. donors. No overhead is charged on contributions; all funds go to work for science, conservation, and education in the Islands.

Endowment contributions can also be made through any of the following organizations, but must be clearly earmarked "for the Galapagos endowment fund:"

> Through the donor's national WORLD WILDLIFE FUND organization.

> WORLD WILDLIFE FUND—U.S.A.
> 1250 Twenty-fourth Street NW
> Washington, DC 20037

> WORLDWIDE FUND FOR NATURE,
> formerly WORLD WILDLIFE FUND
> INTERNATIONAL (WWF International)
> Avenue du Mont Blanc
> CH-1196 Gland, Switzerland

If tax deductions are not sought, contributions may be made directly to:

> CHARLES DARWIN FOUNDATION
> 836 Mabelle
> Moscow, Idaho 83843
> Attention: President, Charles Darwin Foundation

> CHARLES DARWIN FOUNDATION
> Greenstead Hall
> Ongar, Essex
> England
> Attention: Mr. G. T. Corley Smith

> CHARLES DARWIN RESEARCH STATION
> Isla Santa Cruz
> Galapagos, Ecuador
> Attention: Director.

RESIDENT BIRDS

* Galapagos penguin (Spheniscus mendiculus)
* Galapagos albatross (Diomedea irrorata)
  Dark-rumped petrel (Pterodroma phoepygia)
  Audubon's shearwater (Puffinus iherminieri)
  White-vented storm petrel (Oceanites gracilis)
  Wedge-rumped storm petrel (Oceanodroma castro)
* Band-rumped storm petrel (Oceanodroma castro)
  Red-billed tropic bird (Paethon aethereus)
  Brown pelican (Pelicanus occidentalis)
  Blue-footed booby (Sula nebouxii)
  Masked booby (Sula sula)
* Flightless cormorant (Nannopterum harrisi)
  Magnificent frigate bird (Fregata magnificens)
  Great frigate bird (Fregata minor)
  Great blue heron (Ardea herodias)
  Common egret (Casmerodius albus)
  Yellow-crowned night heron (Nyctanassa violacea)
* Lava heron (Butorides sundevalli)
  American flamingo (Phoenocopterus ruber)
* White-cheeked pintail (Anas bahamensis)
  Black rail (Laterallus jamaicensis)
* Galapagos rail (Neocrex erythrops)
  Common gallunule (Gallinula chloropus)
  American oystercatcher (Haematopus palliatus)
  Black-necked stilt (Himantopus mexicanus)
* Lava gull (Larus fulginosa)
* Swallow-tailed gull (Creagus furcatus)

Sooty tern (Stema fuscata)
Brown noddy (Anous stolidus)
* Galapagos dove (Zenaida galapagoensis)
* Dark-billed cuckoo (Coccyzus melacoryphus)
  Barn owl (Tyto alba)
  Short-eared owl (Asio flammeus)
  Vermillion flycatcher (Pyrocephalus rubinus)
* Large-billed flycatcher (Myiarchus magnirostris)
* Galapagos martin (Progne modesta)
* Galapagos mockingbird (Nesomimus parvulus)
* Chatham mockingbird (Nesomimus melanotis)
* Hood mockingbird (Nesomimus macdonaldi)
* Champion mockingbird (Nesomimus trifasci)
* Yellow warbler (Dendroica petechia)
* Warbler finch (Certhidea olivacea)
* Small ground finch (Geospiza fuliginoza)
* Medium ground finch (Geospiza fortis)
* Large ground finch (Geospiza magnirostris)
* Sharp-beaked ground finch (Geospiza diffia)
* Cactus finch (Geospiza scandens)
* Large cactus finch (Geospiza conirostris)
* Small tree finch (Camarhynchus parvulus)
* Medium tree finch (Camarhynchus pauper)
* Large tree finch (Camarhynchus psittacula)
* Vegetarian finch (Platyspiza crassirostris)
* Woodpecker finch (Cactospiza pallida)
* Mangrove finch (Cactospiza heliobates)
* Galapagos hawk (Buteo galapagoensis)

TRANSIENT BIRDS

Sooty shearwater (Puffinus griseus)
Snowy egret (Egrata thula)
Osprey (Pandion haliaetus)
Black-bellied plover (Squaterola squaterola)
Semipalmated plover (Charadrius semi-palma)
Whimbrel (Numenius phaeopus)
Lesser yellowlegs (Totanus flavipes)
Spotted sandpiper (Actis macularia)
Willet (Catoptrophorus semipalmatus)
Wandering tattler (Heteroscelus incanum)
Ruddy turnstone (Arenaria interpres)
Sanderling (Calidris alba)
Least sandpiper (Erolia minutilla)
Wilsons phalarope (Steganopus tricolor)
Northern phalarope (Lobipes lobites)
Laughing gull (Larus aritcilla)
Franklins gull (Larus pipixcan)
Artic tern (Sterna paradisaea)
Royal tern (Sterna maxima)
Barn swallow (Hirundo rustica)
Bobolink (Dolichonyx oryzivorus)

REPTILES

* Galapagos tortoise (Geochelone elephan-topus)
* Galapagos land iguana (Conolophus sub-cristatus)
* Galapagos marine iguana (Amblyrhnus cristatus)
* Galapagos lava lizard (Tropiduris sp.)
* Galapagos snake (Dromicus sp.)
Green pacific turtle (Chelonia mydas)

RESIDENT MAMMALS

* Galapagos bats (Lasiurus brachyotis, L. cinereus)
* Galapagos rats (Oryzomys sp.)
* Galapagos sea-lion (Zalophus califor-nianus wollenbaekii)
* Galapagos fur seal (Archtocephalus aus-tralis galapagoensis)

TRANSIENT MAMMALS

Sperm whale (Physeter catadon)
Fin-back whale (Balaenoptera sp.)
Killer whale (Orcinus orca)
Bottle-nosed dolphin (Tursiops truncatus)
Common dolphin (Delphinus delphis)

FERAL MAMMALS

Cat (Felis felis)
Cattle (Bos taurus)
Dog (Canis canis)
Donkey (Equus asinus)
Goat (Capra hircus)
Mouse (Mus musculus)
Black rat (Rattus rattus)
Pig (Sus scrofa)

* Species endemic to the Galapagos Islands.

Reprinted by permission of the *M/V Bucanero*